LABOUR'S PROMISED LAND?
Culture and Society in Labour Britain 1945–51

LABOUR'S PROMISED LAND?

Culture and Society in Labour Britain 1945–51

edited by
Jim Fyrth

with an introduction by
Victor Kiernan

LAWRENCE & WISHART
LONDON

Lawrence & Wishart Limited
144a Old South Lambeth Road
London SW8 1XX

First published 1995

Photoset in Garamond by
Derek Doyle & Associates, Mold, Clwyd.
Printed and bound in Great Britain by
Redwood Books, Trowbridge.

Contents

CONTENTS

CONTENTS

Preface

This is the second of two collections of essays marking the fiftieth anniversary of Labour's electoral landslide of 1945. The first, *Labour's High Noon: The Government and the Economy 1945–51*, was published in 1993.

That volume analysed different aspects of Labour's economic policies and their consequences. This book explores wider territory, the cultural climate of Labour Britain and the framework of post-war political culture and welfare policies which conditioned that climate. Few histories of the period pay more than superficial attention to cultural developments, although they were of considerable significance.

The essays do not cover every aspect of British culture – there is, for instance, no chapter on science. Their aim is rather to convey to readers in the 1990s the atmosphere – social, political and cultural – in which artists and intellectuals worked. Naturally, there are differences in emphasis and approach among the contributors, because there was no one line of development which embraced all corners of cultural life; there were successes and failures as the hopes of 1945 were fulfilled or disappointed.

It is tempting today, when British society is fragmented and cultural endeavour too often starved or thwarted, to look back at post-war Britain with nostalgia. But these chapters show clearly that, in spite of all that was achieved then, no rosy view of the period is justified. Much of what went well in Britain from the 1950s to the 1970s, as well as much of what went badly, had its source in what was done or not done from 1945–51. Readers of these two volumes may wish to consider if there are things relevant to our own time that may be learned from them.

I am grateful to the many people who have advised me in

putting the two volumes together, and to the workers at Lawrence & Wishart for their support. Especially I wish to thank the contributors, not only for writing, but also for their tolerance in bearing with my importunate editorial demands.

Jim Fyrth, Winter 1994

Notes on Contributors

Catherine Blackford lives and works in London, where she is employed as a Research Assistant at the University of East London. She contributed 'The Best of Both Worlds?: Women's Employment in Post-War Britain' to *Labour's High Noon: The Government and the Economy 1945-51* (Lawrence & Wishart, 1993) and is currently engaged in research for a doctoral thesis on feminism in the 1940s and 1950s.

Douglas Bourn has written numerous articles on the history of the Labour Movement and education and on the history of the Woodcraft Folk for which he worked in the 1970s and 1980s. He has also contributed to journals and seminars on the history of the Co-operative Movement.

John Callaghan is Professor of Politics at the University of Wolverhampton. He is author of *The Far Left in British Politics* (Blackwell, 1987), *Socialism in Britain Since 1884* (Blackwell, 1990) and *Rajani Palme Dutt: A Study in British Stalinism* (Lawrence & Wishart, 1993) and contributed 'In Search of Eldorado: Labour's Colonial Economic Policy' to *Labour's High Noon: The Government and the Economy 1945-51*.

Christine Collette is a Senior Lecturer in Women's Studies at Edge Hill College, Lancashire. Her work on Labour Movement history includes *For Labour and for Women* (Manchester University Press, 1989) and her thesis on Labour

Movement internationalism (Oxford University, 1993). She convenes the Labour Heritage Women's Research Committee which conducts oral history.

Andy Croft teaches Literature and Creative Writing in Middlesbrough for the University of Leeds Department of Adult Continuing Education. He has written a study of novelists and the Popular Front in the 1930s, *Red Letter Days* (Lawrence & Wishart, 1990) and recently abridged J.B. Priestley's *English Journey* for BBC Radio Four. He is currently writing a biography of the poet Randall Swingler.

Rosalind Delmar studied politics at Manchester University. Active in the second wave of feminism, she has contributed to several anthologies on Women's Liberation and Feminism. Other writings include *Joris Ivens: Fifty years of Film-making* (British Film Institute, 1979) and the translation of *A Woman* by Sibilla Aleramo (Virago, 1979). She lectures and writes on the history of feminist ideas and lives in London.

Martin Durham is a Senior Lecturer in Politics at the University of Wolverhampton. He has published a number of essays on the Right in Britain and the USA and is the author of *Sex and Politics: The Family and Morality in the Thatcher Years* (Macmillan, 1991). He is currently working on a study of women and British Fascism.

Roger Fieldhouse is Professor of Adult Education and Director of Continuing Education at the University of Exeter. He was Tutor-Organiser for the WEA in North Yorkshire (1964-70) and Lecturer/Senior Lecturer in the Extramural Department of the University of Leeds (1970-86). He contributed 'Education and Training for the Workforce' to *Labour's High Noon: The Government and the Economy 1945-51*.

Steven Fielding is a Lecturer in the Department of Politics and Contemporary History, University of Salford. He is the author of *Class and Ethnicity: Irish Catholicism in England 1880-1939* (Open University Press, 1993) and has jointly edited *The Wilson Governments 1964-70* (Pinter, 1993) and *Workers' Worlds: Culture and Communites in Manchester and Salford 1880-1940* (Manchester University Press, 1992).

Jim Fyrth was Senior Staff Tutor in History at the University of London Extra-Mural Department. He now teaches for Birkbeck College, London, Extra-Mural Centre. His most recent books are *The Signal Was Spain: The Aid Spain Movement in Britain 1936-39* (Lawrence & Wishart, 1986), (as editor with Sally Alexander) *Women's Voices from the Spanish Civil War* (Lawrence & Wishart, 1991) and (as editor) *Labour's High Noon: The Government and the Economy 1945-51*. He is a Fellow of the Royal Historical Society.

Nigel Glendinning is Emeritus Professor of Spanish at the University of London and an Honorary Fellow of Queen Mary and Westfield College. He has published extensively on Spanish literature, art and architecture, more particularly on Goya, and on the response of artists to the Spanish Civil War.

Steve Iliffe is a General Practitioner in north-west London, and Senior Lecturer in Primary Health Care at University College London Medical School. He was editor of *Medical World*, house journal of the Medical Section of the Manufacturing, Science and Finance Union (MSF) from 1990-94, and is a member of the editorial board of *Health Matters*, the radical health policy journal.

Victor Kiernan is Professor Emeritus in History at the University of Edinburgh. He studied at Manchester Grammar School and Trinity College, Cambridge. He spent several years in India before its Independence. From 1948 until his retirement he belonged to the Department of History at Edinburgh University. He has written widely on a variety of subjects, including European History, imperialism, Marxism and literature.

Robert Looker is a Lecturer in Politics at the University of York. He has written widely on Socialist politics and labour movements and parties. He is currently working on a volume on the Labour Party and the working class in post-war Britain.

Andy Medhurst lectures in the School of Cultural and Community Studies at the University of Sussex where he teaches courses on film, media and popular culture. He writes regularly for *Sight and Sound* and the *Observer*, and is currently researching a book on British film and television comedy.

Steve Parsons teaches History at Sønderborg Gymnasium og HF, Denmark. He took an MA at the Centre for the Study of Social History, University of Warwick in 1981, where his dissertation was on the Communist Party of Great Britain and 1956. He later completed his PhD at the Centre: *Communism in the Professions: the Organisation of the British Communist Party Among Professional Workers* (1990).

Angela Partington is a Lecturer in Cultural Studies and Design History at the University of the West of England, Bristol. She has a doctorate from the University of Birmingham, has published a number of articles on women's relationship to visual culture, and is currently writing a book on twentieth century British design.

Alison Ravetz is Professor Emeritus at Leeds Metropolitan University. She trained as an archaeologist under Gordon Childe and Mortimer Wheeler and started as housing scholar/researcher with *Model Estate* (Croom Helm/ Beckenham 1974) a study of Leeds' Quarry Estate. Her work on the history of planning includes *Remaking Cities* –

Contradictions of the Recent Urban Environment (Croom Helm, Beckenham 1980) and *The Government of Space* (Faber and Faber, London 1986) and her book *The Place of Home: English Domestic Environments 1914–2000* is published by Spon, Andover 1995.

Alan Sinfield is Professor of English in the School of Cultural and Community Studies at the University of Sussex and convenor of the MA programme 'Sexual Dissidence and Cultural Change'. Recent publications include *Faultlines: Cultural Materialism and the Politics of Dissident Reading* (Oxford University Press, 1992), *Cultural Politics – Queer Reading* (Routledge, London 1994) and *The Wilde Century: Effeminacy, Oscar Wilde and the Queer Movement* (Cassell, London 1994).

Jonathan Wood graduated in History at University College, London and was a postgraduate student at Warwick University's Centre for the Study of Social History where he was awarded an MA and a PhD. The subject of his doctoral thesis was 'The Labour Left and the Constituency Labour Parties 1931-1951'.

Introduction: Missing the Tide

Victor Kiernan

> There is a tide in the affairs of men
> Which taken at the flood leads on to fortune;
> Omitted, all the voyage of their life
> Is bound in shallows and in miseries.
>
> William Shakespeare, *Julius Caesar*, Act iv, Scene iii

The years between 1945, when Britain near the end of the Second World War astonished itself by electing a Labour government, and 1951 when this Government was ousted by the Tories and the door to progress closed, can be expected to stand out in future history books as a time of unique opportunity, only very half-heartedly grasped; one of the great historical turning-points at which history failed to turn. There had been nothing like this after the First World War, when Labour was young and its leaders were still more lacking in ardour for change, and in confidence and ability to bring it about.

Labour's Inheritance – a Museum of the Ages

Socialist ideas are very much older than the Labour Party. Without looking back as far as the Middle Ages, we can see them taking shape before the middle of the nineteenth century. The Industrial Revolution brought into being two nearly new, inseparably linked, classes of industrial capitalists and wage-earners. It could not be long before the question began to be asked, whether the new wealth produced by technology should go to enriching a selfish few, or should it be employed for the benefit of people at large? Socialist ideas had more of a welcome in countries such as Germany where industrialism had a more sudden and startling impact. British workers by contrast were learning, after the defeat of their great Chartist movement in the 1840s, to accept social inequality, with very wide differences between rich and poor, as a law of life. There was much trade union activity, but little interest in anything beyond bread and butter issues. Political rights were won, step by step; working-class indifference, or rather deafness, to Socialism made it easy to keep the workers trailing behind the Conservative or the Liberal Party, till as late as 1906.

It was through lack of determination, rather than of opportunity, that the other new class failed to gain the position that it might have had. Reform Acts notwithstanding, the businesspeople were content to go on leaving government and its profits very much in the same hands as before. They relied on the landowners for protection against their discontented workers; it was the aristocracy and landed gentry who controlled the army. Marx expected a collision between an old ruling class and a new one bent on supplanting it, but this never happened. The old one was left its monopoly ownership of the land, and its parasitic revenue from agriculture; it was able to levy tribute on the growing industrial towns, in need of land for building. That truly extraordinary survivor, the House of Lords, and with it the monarchy, remained intact as bastions of conservatism.

This reluctance of the industrial bourgeoisie to deprive the old ruling class of the power it had so long enjoyed and abused, meant that the country's whole structure was developing in a very shuffling, lopsided fashion. Among the gentry, always most at home when jumping over hedges in pursuit of foxes, there was little taste for the vulgar business of running factories and having to wrestle with trade unions.

They, or their younger sons, flocked into the City, and swelled their incomes by assuming ornamental places on railway company boards; others entered the Army and Navy, and conquered dozens of colonies, of which their cousins became governors. Before the end of the last century other countries were industrializing, more rapidly than Great Britain had done, and Germany and the USA were leaving Britain behind, with its economy unhealthily tilted towards finance and foreign investments, instead of productive industry. This imbalance has continued to worsen, with Thatcherism marking its most recent stage. In 1945, the Labour Party had to grapple with this archaic national structure.

To bring ideas of large-scale change into practical politics, in this museum of the ages, a second World War was required. War and its long drawn out strains accentuated working-class consciousness, and also brought the less well-off, less self-complacent sections of the middle classes into agreement on the need of far-reaching reforms. Women assumed new duties and opportunities, and were ready to agitate for their own and other people's rights. It was a remarkable sign of growing political good sense that the country voted against Churchill, who relied on his laurels as Britain's champion against the Nazis; this was a blow crippling enough to keep Toryism quiet for some time. But it was only a beginning, a chance to launch Britain on a new era of planned change. There was no Socialist programme ready to be implemented; aims were limited to social welfare and economic growth. This made them acceptable to middle-class opinion as it was then; but if it had been followed up with enough energy and breadth it could have set the country on a course towards something more radical, a more thorough sweeping out of Augean stables.

Labourism in Practice

According to Leninist doctrine, outsiders have been needed to bring Socialist ideas to the working class. Certainly there has been little sign of any labour movements generating it for themselves, in Britain or elsewhere. In the Labour ministry of 1945-1951 the most progressive member, Aneurin Bevan, came from the working class; but so did the most unprogressive, Ernest Bevin, who was to do harm beyond measuring as the diehard of colonialism and Cold War. But leaders from the upper-middle class had little more notion of bringing Socialism to the Labour Movement. That badge of conservatism, the old school tie, waved like a flag over a field wider than Toryism. *New Statesman* readers must have puzzled one week as to whether its influential editor Kingsley Martin was talking seriously, or facetiously, when he told them that so-and-so could not be given a Cabinet place because that would alter the balance between ex-pupils of one fashionable 'public' school and those of another. Only in England could *Alice in Wonderland* have been written.

Attlee had protested with real feeling at times against the British government's friendliness towards the fascist side in the Spanish War of the 1930s. He had a good deal of kinship, however, with the eighteenth-century Enlightenment reformers whose watchword was 'Everything for the people, nothing by the people'. When Sir Stafford Cripps came to speak at Cambridge before the war a student guard had to be enrolled to protect him from Tory rowdies. He was expelled for a while from the Labour Party for advocating a People's Front against Chamberlain; now, as Chancellor of the Exchequer, he seemed to have no message for ordinary voters except to tighten their belts, and leave good cheer to the millionaires. John Strachey before the war was eloquently spreading the message of Marxism; in 1950-51 he was Secretary for War, sending young conscripts off to colonial wars. 'Bless thee, Bottom, thou art translated!' – as history has had to say to a sad multitude of progressives. A good proportion of both trade union activists and Socialist intellectuals belonged to the Communist Party. It was one feature of a very muddled situation that progressives could often go on being progressive only by going out into a wilderness where they were for most purposes as harmless as monks shut up in their monastery, or lions in their zoo.

A mixed economy would be inevitable. With private enterprise, the policy should have been to encourage firms usefully productive, at the expense, if necessary, of the inessential. Some branches of the economy had to be nationalised. One of the first of these ought to have been land, whose private ownership was merely a burden on those who did the work, and on the consumers of its products. But timidity held Labour back and restricted it to the line of least resistance, nationalising the most sick and least profitable industries. Railways were the most important. In most countries they had been state-built, wholly or partly, from the beginning; in Britain they had been left to private enterprise, with deplorable results, to which the great financial crash of 1847 was the prelude. Nationalisation was simply their transfer to the position they ought always to have had. But they were made to pay the price of their own redemption, which ought to have been paid by the nation, and were very inadequately subsidised. How far workers or managers were fired by a real eagerness to make a success of them, is debatable. The car, pampered rival of the locomotive, was not taken over by the British nation, but was left to be taken over by foreign corporations.

In the 1920s boys were selling newspapers in the streets bare-footed, while there were enough unemployed to make shoes for the whole world. It was high time for something like a Welfare State to be inaugurated. The National Health Service was an essential pillar, and the Labour government's most lasting monument, even if the plans of its designer, Aneurin Bevan, were not fully realised. One obstacle was recalcitrance on the part of doctors. Socialists like Kautsky had from early days hopes of professional workers coming to share their ideals, because it was only in a Socialist commonwealth that their gifts could have full play. But they had mostly proved willing, with lawyers at their head, to take a more humdrum view of motives and vocations. This country had a Socialist Medical Association, active but small.

It has been part of the NHS's strength that its benefits have to a great extent been shared by the middle as well as the working classes; though recently some of the former have shown signs of wanting to desert it, and seek something better for themselves. There must always have been some, in this native land of the snob, who resented the Health Service as too egalitarian. Better health demanded better housing, which raised other intractable problems. Housing estates were designed after scant consultation with the people who were to live there. Most of these would belong to the working classes. Bevan thought there should be a social mixture. This has been experimented with in some towns, among them New York where the oil and vinegar do not seem to have blended well. Some new building did more harm to the countryside than good to the new occupants. Conservation was in its infancy. There was talk of a hundred New Towns – a nightmarish thought in overcrowded Britain.

Pioneers of the Labour Movement had looked to education not for private interest or advancement alone, but as the gateway to social change and emancipation; a notion which during the Cold War invited some suspicion of communistic leanings among teachers. (In those years everything good was unfailingly labelled communist, though nothing communist was labelled good.) Thirst for knowledge failed to spread far in the Labour ranks. A collection of memoirs of self-taught working men in the nineteenth century[1] shows them often feeling cut off from their fellows, looked at askance as freaks. This stemmed from an anti-intellectual twist, not fully banished today, bred by 'Labourism', the *ghettoizing* of the working class, or alienation from the mainstream of national culture. With this has mingled a sort of negative solidarity, a dislike of individuals getting ahead by their book-learning and leaving others behind; an outlook very opposite to that of the smaller, closer-knit Jewish community, to which knowledge really has brought emancipation. Opportunities for adult education were taken up with only limited alacrity. Speakers invited to talk to Workers' Educational Association groups were apt to find most of their listeners middle-class. Now that the workers, or a government put in office by them, were faced with so many complicated problems at home and abroad, their ingrained indifference to anything not under their noses was a grave handicap.

As for schools, those stepping-stones to the future, England had in its grammar schools an old, impressive, and truly meritocratic tradition. A levelling upward towards their academic standards was a choice favoured by many. From the northern counties, their homeland, had come for centuries talents that the backward south, under the deadweight of its fox-hunters, was incapable of breeding. They may have fostered a somewhat too competitive spirit; but even in the most strenuous of them, like the Manchester Grammar School, some infusion of laziness, Lafargue's *droit à la paresse*, could find shelter. The choice fell however on the comprehensive model, with perhaps something like Mao's utopian insistence on China moving towards prosperity at the speed of the slowest, so as to preserve perfect equality.

It must shed some light on the question of what art has meant for humanity that popular interest in it flourished so promisingly during the war, and wilted so quickly after it. A hard-headed, left-wing Scottish engineer carried a complete Shakespeare round the world during war-time, but never opened it again once he got home. A year or so after the war a visitor to remote Lerwick in the Shetlands could meet with an excellent programme of 'Intimate Opera', old ballad operas rendered by a piano and a couple of singers.

At other times there have been sudden flowerings and fading of a home-made culture of the people. During the inter-war slump, a touring theatre movement sprang up in the mining districts of Fife, but then vanished. Tension stimulates, it appears, normality brings back torpor. Interest in art, as in politics, may not come naturally to most of us. People waiting impatiently after the war for houses to be built objected to public money being spent on subsidies to cultural enterprises like the Edinburgh Festival. On the other hand, various critics then and later have blamed the Labour government for giving too little help to the arts. Helping them would have been a very intricate task for any government to undertake. It may be admitted all the same, that this one had a strong vein of philistinism, whether more among those from the ranks of labour or from outside them, or shared evenly by both.

Hanging on to Empire

In the Government's international and colonial policies we can see most clearly of all how very imperfect was its readiness to break with the past. John Saville has studied the foreign policies of the time; and shown how Ernest Bevin as Foreign Minister trumpeted his intentions at the outset by sending troops to help the French restore their hated rule in Vietnam, and for the Dutch to do the same in Indonesia, for fear of sparks of colonial revolt spreading to British possessions[2] – 'the jolly old Empire', in his elegant phrase. Britain was obliged to give up India in 1947, as well as Burma and Ceylon, and it does seem to have been understood that the other territories could not be held indefinitely by force. But they would be kept as long as possible, and means would be devised to keep them subservient even after de-colonization.

This has been brought to light, with much striking confirmation from the archives, in two recent books by Frank Füredi.[3] Harold Wilson, who was regarded as being on the left-wing of the party, is quoted as declaring in 1949 that no party could monopolize 'the title Imperialist in the best sense of the word'. It must be added that Labour was, or thought itself, obliged to go on working through the officials entrenched in the Foreign and Colonial Departments, practically all of them Tories, many in the worst sense of the word.

Shortly before the riots at Accra in the Gold Coast (now Ghana) in 1948, Creech-Jones the Colonial Secretary was pledging 'firm and resolute' action to keep West Africa under control. In Malaya and Kenya firmness was to lead to protracted and very costly military operations. Jungle fighting took something like 30,000 man-hours of army time to catch and kill one guerrilla. World opinion was hostile; as was, in the early stages, the American government, which wanted to take over Britain's place in the world. London had to fall back on the plea that the colonies, especially in Africa, were not yet ready for self-rule, but were being trained and prepared for it as quickly as possible. Determination to keep an empire went with resolve to keep Britain a first-rate power, with the help of H-bombs. This meant reckless squandering of scarce resources, and reduced Britain to dependence on the USA; it was compelled to join in the Cold War, and in the civil war in Korea, and the propaganda battle against the USSR, so recently Europe's liberator from the Nazis. A cartoonist once depicted the 'special relationship' hankered for by Britons as a servitor obsequiously kneeling to present a trencher of meat to a lordly person seated at a banqueting table.

In return, Washington toned down its criticisms of British colonial conduct, and helped London cope with some of its troubles; the more readily because Britain could now lay the blame for any colonial discontents on agents of Moscow. Meanwhile the Colonial Office was elaborating, as Füredi shows in detail, a strategy of harassing and isolating colonial leaders judged to be honest and unbribable, and aiding and abetting the more 'moderate' or self-seeking careerists who could be trusted to submit to British leading-strings. One after another men like Nkrumah in the Gold Coast gave way and agreed to expel the left-wing from their movements, as the Labour Party in Great Britain had been so ready to do, and thereby deprived their parties of most of their vitality. In this good work the TUC was easily got to lend a helping hand, like a tame elephant helping its masters to catch and train a wild one. Few in Britain raised any objection, except the Communists, who went unheard.

These manoeuvres had considerable success; so that when the Tories returned to power they could before long give up their imperial tub-thumping and – as David Goldsworthy showed a few years ago – march their bemused followers backwards out of Africa and elsewhere.[4] It has become a fashion to excuse Imperialism as really the outcome of would-be collaborators in regions like India wanting powerful foreigners as partners. It was in fact the other way about; but at this later stage it may be said that the requirement was mutual. Collaborators were carefully picked out, and licked into shape. The result was that many emancipated colonies, as in other empires too, had to start their new lives with the handicap of bosses chosen for them from outside; the consequences have too often been what could easily be expected. Harder to comprehend, in any rational terms, is what motives made the colonialists want to leave their territories in such a condition, with Britannia looking like an impoverished Highland chieftain of old, proud of her long 'tail' of ragamuffin followers.

War Weariness and Demagogy

We can only speculate as to how much the Labour government could have achieved if it had been made of sterner stuff, and how different Britain and the world might be today. There was no energetic enough mass feeling to stiffen the flagging leadership. Long years of war, crisis and tumult had spread weariness of everything outside the narrow radius of private interests. During the war the famous batsman Walter Hammond called on the country to work for speedy victory, so that it could settle down again to playing cricket. Among students, many of them ex-servicemen and women, Existentialism was in vogue in the years after 1945, a development which Marxists viewed with a jaundiced eye, but was quite natural. After a desperate war, people are glad to have survived, and very conscious of each of us having only one life, and wanting to savour it.

This state of mind made an ideal target for the upper-class demagogy of which England has long made a speciality; first among middle-class voters sympathetic for a time to the reforms, but not them alone: after all, in the inter-war years the working class itself had given half its votes to the Tory 'National Government'. Demagogy can be seen unfolding its blandishments in the English history-plays of that keen student of politics, William Shakespeare, or in the shrewd advice bestowed by wealthy friends on Coriolanus, as a candidate for the consulship, which he could easily win by a little flattery and cajolery of the citizens. 'Set the People Free' – from restrictions and regulations dictated by shortages – was one Tory slogan. With charming impudence a poster exclaimed: 'Don't just grumble at the Socialists – get rid of them!' It must have been a permanent cause of humanity's sluggish advance that only great crises and catastrophes can kindle strong desire for change, but the same tempests exhaust nervous resources, and make humanity incapable of the effort of bringing about what it desires. A few are ready to push on, most drop out. Momentum has been best maintained by coercion, as it was in Stalin's impressive re-building of Russia after 1945 – which within not very many years petered out in weariness and stagnation.

In 1951 the Tories were restored to power. Once again Britain was being weighed in the balance and found wanting. In 1952 there was a vulgarly histrionic coronation, amid floods of appalling oratory about Britain dedicating itself afresh to its mission and its semi-sacred monarchy. All this represented a culmination for which Labour ministers had prepared the way, like John the Baptist in the wilderness, convinced that the people needed nothing so much as a liberal dose of State pageantry to help them forget the war. Most of the coronation hubbub would be forgotten within a week; but some dregs of the synthetic enthusiasm so elaborately manufactured would linger on and clog many people's minds. On the plane of workaday reality the classes, as Harold Macmillan when premier was uneasily aware, were drifting further apart.

Labour had worked its six days of Creation, and then in 1951 stopped to rest, as it has been doing, broadly speaking, ever since. After an election victory Harold Wilson was photographed, pipe in mouth and feet up on a big Downing Street desk, informing a pressman that what the country wanted was not a new programme, but just better administration.

From Butskellism to Thatcherism

It seems strange now that so many socialists in those years should have taken for granted, in spite of many disappointments and the Cold War, that the gains made were irreversible; that private greed would never be able to lay its hands again on Britain's railways, or attempt to subvert the Health Service. Some optimism was allowable. Hitler was dead, Thatcherism had not yet been born. There was a Tory MP, Sir Waldron Smithers, personifying prehistoric beliefs of all kinds, but he was only thought of as a gift from heaven to the cartoonists. It became a habit to talk of 'Butskellism', or a hybrid mixture of the ideas of moderate conservatism like R.A. Butler's and very moderate demi-semi-socialism like Hugh Gaitskell's; an inert compound likely to do little good but not very much harm. But underneath such soporifics there was lurking true-blue Toryism in sheep's clothing, which in due course would be ready to bare its Thatcherite teeth and snarl.

Privatisation has been the grand affair of the last dozen years, bringing changes that threaten to prove more irreversible than any brought about by Labour. It has been the modern English equivalent of what has accompanied many great upheavals of the past: seizures and sales to the monied classes of public or nationalised property. This happened with the Reformation everywhere, the English civil wars, the bourgeois revolutions in France, Spain, Italy. Privatisation has been a gigantic bribe to the middle classes with money to invest, and a handsome reward to the Tory organizers themselves. They were under no obligation, as they ought to have been, either to practise self-denial or to admit that they were taking their share of the spoils.

This has robbed the nation, and widened the gap between the better-off classes and the rest. It has also helped to worsen the obsession with financial gambling and trickery, the neglect of useful industry, from which Britain has so long suffered. When manufactures dwindled, while in other countries they expanded, Mrs Thatcher light-heartedly left it to the 'service industries' to take up the slack. English people in other words could pay their way by polishing the shoes of prosperous foreigners visiting London. Two House of Commons committees, mainly Tory, have been opening their eyes belatedly to the effect on the national economy, a Britain left with less and less to export except guns and bombs, and more and more need to import. Socialists do well to find fault with capitalism of any sort, but Britain's particular plague is having too little of the more active kind of capitalism. A pseudo-capitalist ruling class faces a pseudo-socialist opposition.

In the post-war years it was assumed all round that if unemployment ever again reached one million, no government could survive; just as in old Turkey a ministry could be expected to fall if the price of coffee went up to a certain point. Tory rule has now survived for a long time with nearly three million unemployed, and has benefited by the Labour Movement being increasingly divided between those with jobs and those without. In contrast, workers in the defeated countries, after 1945 under foreign occupation, were given work to do, and worked hard, the more willingly because their employers were kept in line, prodded, and shepherded by governments bent on economic growth, instead of being left to straggle and stray as they pleased, or to pause for a round of golf, or a friendly chat with their secretaries. German trade unionists have been investing their funds in the enterprises they work for. British workers have fallen between two stools, neither trying to replace capitalism with something better nor willing to make friends with it.

Instead of social revolution, the frustration of after-the-war hopes has had a share in bringing about, as a poor consolation-prize, a sexual revolution, or slide into promiscuity and commercial exploitation. The family, which conservatives had always claimed as the ark of their covenant, has been more or less jettisoned. Tories have had more serious things – stock exchange profits – to think of, and have been happy to see the country turning away from serious thinking to something easier. The velocity of circulation among the amorous has quickened yearly. Religion has been fading at the same rate. It may teach the respectable classes how to lay up treasure in heaven, but Mrs Thatcher has taught them how to lay up treasure on earth, at the expense of their poorer neighbours, and they have given her their vote.

So startling has the contrast become between sluggish Britain and its dynamic competitors that the more benighted Tories are anxious now to escape out of Europe, and get the British public to forget that there are places where things are better done, and workers are better paid. Britain's entry into Europe, bringing to an end, as Gaitskell said, an island history of a thousand years, looked at first suspiciously like a manoeuvre to reinforce Toryism with European partners, as the Cold War alliance with America had reinforced it – or, further back, James I's entente with catholic Spain. But as things have turned out, Europe has in many ways given Britain a shove forward instead of back: the European Union is at least businesslike enough to make room for reforms necessary for social and economic growth. Our government has preferred the easier short cuts of giving profiteers and developers and take-over bidders a free hand. Once more Tories are 'setting the people free', this time from European standards and regulations, with no regard for health or safety or minimum living standards. In the past few years there has been a symbolic spread of food-poisoning.

But capitalism the world over suffers from maladies that must increasingly undermine it. They are moral as well as material. Corruption, clandestine bargainings between plutocrats and politicians, have always been rampant in America, Japan, and elsewhere; now they are world-wide. At the opposite pole, in this country, at any rate, the spirit of progress and welfare is being privatised, or discarded by a government resolved to do nothing good if it can possibly avoid it, and is left to voluntary workers for good causes, of whom we can be grateful for having a large number. Among them we may hope to see more and more of Gramsci's 'organic intellectuals' of labour taking their places, men and women equal in education to any from the middle classes, but still cherishing the radical feelings of the old Labour Movement.

Much progressive energy has to be devoted to fending off the harm done by a government without a conscience and those who keep it in power. We cannot expect capitalism to give up willingly its cannibal diet of whales and forests and human beings. Their defence, conservation on all fronts, may prove in default of any royal highway to a more civilised future, a valuable, though roundabout, road.

Notes

[1] David Vincent, *Bread, Knowledge and Freedom: A Study of Nineteenth-Century Working Class Autobiography*, Methuen, London 1981.
[2] John Saville, *The Politics of Continuity: British Foreign Policy and the Labour Government 1945-46*, Verso, London 1993; and 'Introduction' to J.

Fyrth (ed), *Labour's High Noon: The Government and the Economy 1945-51*, Lawrence & Wishart, London 1993; see also P.S. Gupta, 'Imperialism and the Labour Government of 1945-51' in Jay Winter, *The Working Class in Modern British History*, Cambridge University Press, Cambridge 1983.

[3] Frank Füredi, *Colonial Wars and the Politics of Third World Nationalism*, I.B. Taurus, London 1994; and *The New Ideology of Imperialism*, Pluto Press, London 1994.

[4] David Goldsmith, *Colonial Issues in British Politics 1945-61*, Clarendon Press, Oxford 1971.

Part 1 – The Post-War Political Culture

Days of Hope: The Meaning of 1945

Jim Fyrth

> But those days we lived, as I tell you, a life that was not our
> own;
> And we saw but the hope of the world, and the seed that the
> ages have sown,
> Spring up now a fair-blossomed tree from the earth lying over
> the dead.
>
> William Morris, Meeting the War Machine,
from The Pilgrims of Hope, 1886

The General Election results were announced on 26 July
1945. For some it was as though the sky had fallen. Winston
Churchill, on hearing the extent of Labour's victory, 'turned
quite grey in his bath'; Oliver Lyttleton, his wartime Minister
of Production, later recalled how, 'I began to fear for my
country'; the right-wing Conservative MP, Sir Henry
('Chips') Channon, recorded that he was 'shocked and
stunned by the country's treachery'. But for others it was a
moment of great hope. Such, it is said, was the euphoria
among the troops in Cairo that for ten days they stopped
saluting officers. Felicity and Alison Attlee joined hands and
danced down Oxford Street when they saw in an evening
paper that their father was Prime Minister. Many were caught
unawares. Hugh Dalton expected, 'either a small Tory
majority or a deadlock'; Harold Nicholson wrote in his diary,
'Nobody foresaw this at all'.[1]

Nobody? From 1943 onwards every opinion poll and
survey showed that the voters had swung to Labour. In four
of the very few by-elections, Conservatives, some in 'safe'

seats, had been defeated by radical Commonwealth or Independent Socialist candidates.[2] Nor could anyone who knew the mood of men and women in war industry or the forces have doubted that a change in the way they saw the world had taken place. This was more than a swing to Labour in electoral terms. There was no great confidence in the Labour leaders, in spite of their competence as Ministers in the Coalition government;[3] the Labour Party in the country was quiescent during the electoral truce, and the national swing to Labour in 1945, compared with the previous General Election in 1935, was only 12 per cent. (It would certainly have been more had more of the men and women in the forces voted – less than half of them did so.[4])

More significant than the electoral swing was the mood that 'things are going to be very different after the war, whoever is in government'. The story of the soldier embarking for the Normandy landings, who called to Ernest Bevin, 'We're not coming back to the dole, Ernie', may be apochryphal, but it summed up a feeling that there would be trouble if 'we' did.

The New Mood

Between the wars Britain was dominated by Conservatism. Labour held office, not very effectively, for only two brief periods, each time by grace of the Liberals. In British society a conservative moral and cultural dominance was all-pervading. Then, during the war, the tide turned and, by 1945, threatened to overwhelm this conservative hegemony with a flood of progressive and radical ideas and, giving these ideas popular power, an emotional desire for a new and better Britain. The core of this challenge was a mixture of Socialist, Labour, Keynesian, Fabian/Liberal and anti-Fascist ideas that was strongly anti-establishment and anti-capitalist, and was hostile to those who were held responsible for poverty and unemployment and for appeasement of the Fascist dictators. This 'Popular Front of the mind' had no agreed central ideology, which was a strength in that it drew support from many diverse directions. But the absence of a theoretical core was to make it brittle under the pressures of the late 1940s. In 1945 and 1946, however, it looked as though Conservative supremacy in society might be quite overthrown and a new hegemony of the Left be established, especially as the tide was flowing leftward right across Europe. But this did not happen, for reasons explored in this book and its companion volume (*Labour's High Noon: The Government and the Economy 1945-51*). What emerged was a consensus between right-wing Labour and progressive Conservatism. Labour was unwilling to challenge the real seats of power in State and society. Conservatism reflected the political wisdom of the British ruling classes who have traditionally known that, to avoid the fate of the Bourbons, it is necessary for them to bend before political and social gales so that they may stand upright again when the wind stops blowing. By the 1970s it had ceased to blow.

Many reasons have been suggested for the new radical mood.[5] The war had taken people out of their ruts, had thrown them together in unaccustomed jobs in unusual places where they had heard new ideas and seen that there were other ways of living. They had learned that they didn't have to put up with the way 'things' were before, and that those who gave the orders were often incompetent. Such a social upheaval happens in any war. But this was not 'any' war. For millions it was a war against Fascism and for Democracy, in alliance with the Soviet Union, which was very popular, the Americans, who were not as popular, and resistance movements, often Communist-led, in occupied countries.

Unbelievable as it may seem now, this was a time when cinema audiences applauded when Stalin or the Red Army appeared on the news-reels and when 'tanks for Russia' weeks could enthuse factory workers; a time when a Tory MP and his wife presided over a British-Soviet Society dance, dressed as Russian peasants, and when an Army General chose to sit down with a Communist lance-corporal to discuss the policy of the Communist Party.[6] The Coalition government was so worried that solidarity campaigns with the Soviet Union might create too much sympathy with Communism, that it decided the campaigns must be led by the establishment itself.[7]

This was not the 'People's War' of mythology, with a united people standing behind Churchill and bearing every sacrifice with a smile. There was looting in the blitz, strikes in the coalfields and there was much justified unrest among merchant seamen. There were also 60,000 conscientious objectors, nearly four times the number of the First World War.[8] But it was a 'People's War' in the sense that, for the first time, very many people were able to exercise influence and make decisions in the workplaces and wartime organisations in which they found themselves, in a way that would have been unthinkable in the 1914-18 War. New forms of democratic participation developed in shelter committees, fire-watching units, Civil Defence, the Home Guard and the voluntary organisations. In 1941 the Amalgamated Engineering Union (AEU) and the General and Municipal Workers' Union (GMWU) called for Joint Production Committees (JPCs) in war industry. In spite of opposition from employers' organisations, by the end of the War JPCs, or their equivalent, had, with government backing, been set up in workplaces employing some three-and-a-half million workers.[9] Tens of thousands of working people were involved in discussing matters which had hitherto been considered the preserve of management.

The rulers of Britain had owed much of their power to the deference which they were able to command in those over whom they ruled. Deference was fuelled by feelings of inferiority and incompetence outside their own sphere among working people.[10] But between 1940 and 1945 thousands of ordinary men and women discovered confidence, independence and stature in forms of democratic participation – and even in the Armed Forces.

A People's Culture

One element which helped to build the confidence and stir the imagination of those touched by it, was the wartime popularisation of culture described below by Andy Croft. In a climate where 'Other Ranks' packed the Catterick Garrison Theatre to watch *Twelfth Night*, and the London Philharmonic Orchestra sold tickets through trade union branches, many realised that the worlds of theatre and music were not for 'Them' only, 'We' had a right to enjoy them too.

This 'People's Culture' of wartime had its roots in the 1930s, when a widening liberal culture had overlapped with the left-wing culture of the 'People's Front' years. A number of initiatives had given a new public access to the arts and brought ideas to many who had previously not met with them. Foremost among these developments were the launching of Penguin Books and the non-fiction Pelicans,[11] and the growth of film societies showing French, Soviet and pre-Hitler German films as well as the products of the documentary movement. With the spread of the wireless, symphony, chamber and other music came into homes where it had rarely been heard, and the BBC Talks Department carried ideas where they had not gone before.[12]

All these were principally enjoyed by those whose education or circumstances made them receptive. The difference in the wartime cultural movement was that it consciously set out to bring drama, music and art to those who previously might well have scorned to cross the road to sample them. This departure owed much to the left-wing culture of the late 1930s, when films, books, pamphlets, plays and pageants were produced to stir opinion against Fascism, war, poverty and unemployment, and to win support for Republican Spain. This 'People's Front' culture had many centres. Victor Gollancz's Left Book Club, launched in 1936, issued a monthly book costing half-a-crown (12½ p) to 58,000 members by 1939. These were discussed in 1200 groups; the club held meetings in the largest halls, sold a million pamphlets and campaigned for Spain, for Czechoslovakia and for deep air-raid shelters. Unity Theatre introduced Brecht, Lorca and Odets to British audiences, produced political plays and 'Living Newspapers' on issues of the moment, and in the winter following the Munich Agreement, a popular political pantomime, *Babes in the Wood*. *Left Review* became the main literary journal on the left, with contributions from almost every writer of note who stood left of centre. The left-wing publishing houses of Gollancz and Martin Lawrence provided a stream of opinion-making books. Gollancz combined non-fiction such as G.D.H. Cole's *Intelligent Man's Guide Through World Chaos* and Alan Hutt's *This Final Crisis* with best selling fiction such as A.J. Cronin's *The Stars Look Down* and *The Citadel*. The first was a criticism of private coalowners, the other of private medicine. Martin Lawrence made the writings of Marx, Lenin and other Socialists available to a wide audience for the first time.[13]

Both the liberal and left-wing cultures contributed to the wartime cultural surge, and helped to popularise ideas which fuelled the leftward swing. Some of the most important wartime publications preparing the way for the Labour victory were the small books in blue covers with bright yellow wrappers, issued by Gollancz between 1940 and 1945; *Guilty Men* by 'Cato' (Michael Foot) sold more than 200,000 copies and was followed by *Your MP* by 'Gracchus', *Why Not Trust the Tories?* by 'Celticus' (Aneurin Bevan) and *The Trial of Mussolini* by 'Cassius' which sold more than 121,000 copies. Others were written by Konni Zilliacus and Emmanuel Shinwell. These vigorous polemics circulated in tens of thousands among service men and women and among factory workers. Documentary films made by the Ministry of Information (MOI) could carry an equally rousing message. *Children of the City*, made by Paul Rotha in 1944, showed the awful housing conditions in Dundee producing child crime and ended, 'We must make it as exciting for our children to build this new world, as is the present temptation to destroy the world of their parents'. And there were many such films.[14]

Plans

This outpouring of ideas contributed massively to Labour's 1945 victory. But the practical programme of the new Government was based not on left-wing ideas but on plans and reports, many of which also had their genesis in the 1930s, and had taken a definite form, and in some cases been legislated, during the war.

Most of these plans, apart from those for nationalisation, came from outside the Labour Party; although the Socialist Medical Association (affiliated to the Labour Party) promoted plans for a health service. The Beveridge Report (1942) was largely the work of the Liberal Sir William Beveridge, although the Socialist G.D.H. Cole had a hand in preparing it. Plans for family allowances originated in the Family Endowment Society in 1917 and the Children's Minimum Council, with the Independent MP Eleanor Rathbone as their principal champion. Wartime nutrition policies were the result of a series of reports on the food and health of the people made between the wars, which showed the extent of malnutrition and the links between poverty and ill health, especially among children. The most influential of many were those of Seebohm Rowntree in York (1934-5) and Sir John Boyd Orr's *Food, Health and Income* (1936).[15] Post-war economic policy owed most to the 'Cambridge School', headed by John Maynard Keynes who was a Liberal with no sympathy for the Labour Party, though some of his disciples were Labour supporters; but progressive Conservatives also advocated a controlled capitalist economy, among them Harold Macmillan in *The Middle Way* (1938).

There was a spate of wartime reports. The Reid Committee Report of 1944 was the blueprint for the nationalisation of the coal industry. The Percy Report (1944) called for a doubling of output of engineering graduates, the Barlow Report (1946) for a doubling of scientists and technologists. The Uthwatt Report on Land-use (1942) recommended a form of land nationalisation. Not all these reports led anywhere, but they created the climate in which post-war policies were made.

People

One of the changes brought by the war was that it was possible more than ever before for leftward looking people to hold positions of influence and authority. One thinks, among many others, of Keynesian economists such as James Meade and Richard Stone in Whitehall, of scientists Desmond Bernal and Solly Zuckerman on Mountbatten's Staff and of Tom Wintringham and Hugh Slater, both of whom had fought in the International Brigades in Spain, commanding the Osterley Park Training School for the Home Guard. Half of the daily press was on the left, and there were a number of influential left-wing journalists.[16] When Frank Owen, the editor of the London *Evening Standard* was called up he was succeeded by Michael Foot, while Owen edited *SEAC*, the progressive forces newspaper in the Far East. E.H. Carr, the historian of the Russian Revolution, edited *The Times* (one Tory MP called it 'the threepenny edition of the *Daily Worker*'); the journalist Frank O'Connor, as 'Cassandra' wrote a popular column in the *Daily Mirror*, which Churchill wanted banned. W.E. Williams, the Pelican Books editor, was Director of the Army Bureau of Current Affairs (ABCA) and there were many left-wing officers on the staffs of Army Education colleges. A Communist, Montagu Slater, was head of filmscripts for the Ministry of Information.

Influential as such people were, the main work of spreading ideas in the factories, Forces and Civil Defence was done by men and women engaged in those spheres. Some gave ABCA lectures or just talked about what was wrong with British society and what should be done about it, and passed round

Through this network they spread ideas and circulated publications among those with whom they served.[18]

Not everyone met or listened to these various left-wing crusaders but their ideas rippled outwards helping to create a widespread emotional desire for radical change. The Labour Party was the inheritor of this mood rather than the creator.

Promised Land?

None, especially in the bleak 1990s, should underestimate the improvements made in the lives of millions by the Labour government. Nor should we forget its cultural achievements, among them the establishment of the National Parks, and the Festival of Britain, that last flowering of wartime togetherness before the Tory government closed it down. The foundation was laid, too, for the growth of musical education which made Britain a world centre for music, and is now being eroded. No doubt a Conservative government would have instituted reforms, but these would have been unlikely to have been so far reaching as those of Labour. Yet before it lost office in 1951 the Government had moved to the right, and Labour was to hold office for only ten of the next forty years.

Why, in spite of its reforms, did Labour lose office? The easy answer is that it lost votes from middle-class people fed up with bread rationing, whale meat and power cuts, and from working class men angry about the 'wage freeze'.[19] We would then have to see the connection between the austerity and wages policy on the one hand and defence spending, and the policies it reflected, on the other. But there was something more.

I have argued that the meaning of 1945 was that Labour benefited from a surge of progressive ideas and radical emotions which had challenged Conservative supremacy throughout society and laid the foundations for a new left hegemony. I have argued also that culture, in both the narrower and wider sense, contributed significantly to this surge. If this is so, it seems to follow that the meaning of 1951 was that the social forces which built these foundations had been defeated and dispersed.

On VE Day Churchill sent a telegram to the British Chargé D'affaires in Moscow, in which he said, '... It is no longer desired by us to maintain detailed arguments with the Soviet Union about their views and actions'. (The Red Army was still fighting the Germans in Czechoslovakia). Within two years the Cold War had turned sympathy for the Soviet Union and what it stood for into hostility. The consequence was a split in the Labour Party with attacks by the Labour leaders both on their own Left and on militant trade unionists. A 'witch-hunt' was launched against Communists and 'fellow travellers', discussed below by Steve Parsons. The divisions on the left were added to by the uncritical support of all Soviet policies by the Communist Party itself, and its increasing isolation. The result was the growing disillusionment of many of those who, in wartime, had crusaded for a Socialist Britain. They may have voted Labour in 1950 and 51 but they were no longer campaigning as enthusiastically as they did in 1945, and no longer had a vision for a 'New Britain'.

The Cold War also spelt the end of that 'Popular Front of the mind', through which, from the late 1930s, Socialists of all kinds, Liberals, progressive and patriotic Conservatives, anti-Fascists and peace campaigners had moved British politics to the left. The 'People's Culture' of wartime gave way to one which was increasingly élitist and metropolitan. Forms of democratic participation created in the war withered as the institutions of Labour Britain became increasingly bureaucratic. Inevitably British politics moved to the right and, by 1950, the ideas which guided Labour were coming from the Croslands and Gaitskells, no longer from the Bevans and Foots.

It was not all the fault of Labour. Millions of men and women wanted to leave everything to do with the war behind them and build their lives, now made more comfortable by full employment and the Welfare State. It can also be argued that given the policies of the American and Soviet governments, the unpleasant consequences of the Cold War were inescapable. But this would overlook the British role in launching the Cold War and the irrationality of the Government's feud against the Left. Nor did the Government attempt to continue the forms of participatory democracy or popular culture that had developed in wartime.

The tragedy of post-war British society was that, in spite of Labour's many achievements, culture and intellectual influence in Britain once more flourished in a walled garden. There were more people in the garden than before 1939 and access was less difficult than in the past; and those outside the garden lived better, with better health care, education and housing. Nevertheless the great majority were outside; the wall was still there and the name of the angel who guarded the gate with a flaming sword was 'Class'.

Notes

[1] Churchill, Capt. Richard Pym, quoted Martin Gilbert, *Never Despair, Winston S. Churchill, 1945-65*, Heinemann, London 1988, p111; Lyttelton, *Memoirs*, quoted Andrew Davies, *Where did the Forties Go?*, Pluto, London 1984, p70; Channon, R. Rhodes James (ed), *Chips, the Diaries of Sir Henry Channon*, Penguin, Harmondsworth 1970, p499; Cairo, Richard Kisch, *The Days of the Good Soldiers*, Journeyman, London 1985, p111; Felicity Attlee, quoted in Peter Hennessy, *Never Again*, Cape, London 1992, p86; Dalton, Hugh Dalton, *The Fateful Years, Memoirs 1931-45*, Muller, London 1957, p466; Nicholson, S. Olsen (ed), *Harold Nicholson, Diaries and Letters 1930-64*, Penguin, Harmondsworth 1980, p292.

[2] R. Sibley, 'The Swing to Labour during the Second World War: When and Why', *Labour History Review*, Vol. 55, Part 1, 1990; Paul Addison, *The Road to 1945*, Cape, London 1975, Quartet, London 1977, pp248-9; Angus Calder and Dorothy Sheridan, *Speak for Yourself*, Cape, London 1984, pp210-17.

[3] Calder and Sheridan, *op.cit.*, p215.

[4] Of 4.53 million in the Forces only 2.9 million went through the complicated procedure of registering and arranging for proxy or postal votes. Of these only 1.7 million voted. It is possible that the increased Labour vote in 1950 owed something to exservice people who had not

voted in 1945.
[5] Some of these are listed in R. Sibley, *op.cit.*
[6] The MP was Sir Philip Colfox (West Dorset). The incident involving the lance-corporal occurred at Ahmednagar when General in Command Southern Signals (India) was inspecting the unit in which the writer served, which was preparing for the Malayan landings against the Japanese.
[7] See P. Addison, *op.cit.*, pp134-40.
[8] Blitz, Calder and Sheridan, *op.cit*, p99; strikes, Angus Calder, *The People's War*, Cape, London 1969, Panther, London 1971, pp507ff; MN, Tony Lane, *The Merchant Seamen's War*, Manchester University Press, 1990.
[9] Calder, *People's War, op.cit.*, pp459-61; Richard Croucher, *Engineers at War*, Merlin, London 1982.
[10] These feelings were finely described by D.H. Lawrence, for instance in his short story *The Daughters of the Vicar*.
[11] The editors of Pelican books, Lance Beales, Reader in Economic History at the London School of Economics, W.E. Williams of the British Institute of Adult Education and Lancelot Hogben, author of the popular guides *Science for the Citizen* and *Mathematics for the Million*, were all leftward looking. Their first publication was Bernard Shaw's *Intelligent Woman's Guide to Socialism, Capitalism, Sovietism and Fascism*.
[12] During the Spanish Civil War (1936-39), a majority of the BBC talks printed in the *Listener* were sympathetic to the Republican government, see Jim Fyrth, *The Signal Was Spain: The Aid Spain Movement in Britain 1936-39*, Lawrence & Wishart, London 1986.
[13] For an account of the left culture of the 1930s see Jon Clark *et al* (eds), *Culture and Crisis in Britain in the Thirties*, Lawrence & Wishart, London 1979; Andy Croft, *Red Letter Days*, Lawrence & Wishart, London 1990; Bert Hogenkamp, *Deadly Parallels: Film and the Left in Britain 1929-39*, Lawrence & Wishart, London 1986; Colin Chambers, *The Story of Unity Theatre*, Lawrence & Wishart, London 1989.
[14] Andy Ferns, *Causes of Change in MOI Film Policy, 1939-45*, Scotland, unpub., 1985, courtesy of author.
[15] For 1930s contributions to welfare ideas see Pat Thane, *The Foundations of the Welfare State*, Longmans, London 1982, pp163ff.
[16] Addison, *op.cit.*, pp151-3.
[17] See Nina Fishman, *The British Communist Party and the Trade Unions 1933-45*, Scolar Press, Aldershot 1994. Local history studies are needed on the CP in war industry before a complete and accurate picture can be drawn.
[18] See, for example, R. Kisch, *op.cit.*; Bill Moore and George Barnsby (eds) *The Anti-Fascist People's Front in the Armed Forces, the Communist Contribution 1939-46*, CP History Group pamphlet 81, London 1990.
[19] See James Hinton, 'Women and the Labour Vote 1945-50', *Labour History Review*, Vol 27, Part 3, 1992.

15

'To Make Men and Women Better Than They Are': Labour and the Building of Socialism

Steven Fielding

We have to make Socialists to whom the spirit of Socialism will mean something in their Labour Party work and in their personal contacts; to make the Labour Party not only a vote winning machine, but something great and glorious that stands for a new way of life. Socialism cannot live and prosper by the winning of elections alone. For one of our purposes is to make men and women better than they are, and to promote 'sweetness and light'.

Herbert Morrison, 1951.[1]

When Labour won its first parliamentary majority in 1945 many within the Party considered that the country had taken an irreversible step towards Socialism. Living now in what has been described as a 'post-socialist era', in which Labour after its 1992 defeat was thought unelectable, such a feeling is hard to credit.[2] This chapter recalls how Party members thought that Socialism was imminent, why and how they thought it would emerge, how they understood the problems of what they saw as the transition between capitalism and

16

Socialism, and how failure to build a socialist society was rationalised.

The Socialist Goal

Before the Second World War it was a matter of abiding faith within Labour's ranks that all roads eventually led to Socialism. This was clearly expressed by Clement Attlee in *The Labour Party in Perspective*, published after the two disastrous general election defeats of 1931 and 1935. Even these defeats failed to dent his belief in the march of progress. He actually felt that the 'objective' economic preconditions for Socialism were already in place in 1930s Britain. Capitalism, he wrote, was manifestly failing; the only obstacle was a popular lack of imagination. Socialism by this stage was simply a question of moral will.[3] The war was seen as improving the prospects for Socialism immeasurably. Not only did it ensure that the economic pre-conditions were even more firmly in place but, more importantly, it transformed popular attitudes.[4] The struggle with Germany was seen as providing the British people with that missing high purpose necessary for the creation of Socialism. Just as they had produced a common effort in the face of common danger so, it was hoped, the people would do the same for the common interest in peacetime.[5]

That the British people had been morally improved by the experience of war was seemingly indicated by the election of a Labour government in 1945.[6] The *Daily Herald* announced that:

> A whole world has died ... It was a world in which private interests were allowed to lord it over the community, a world in which Britain's position was steadily undermined by tolerance of industrial inefficiency and moral decline.
>
> The war was won by the British people's resolve to break with these bad traditions. They have made it clear to all the

world that they are ready to transform our country into a Socialist Commonwealth.[7]

1945 was, therefore, considered to be much more than a simple election triumph. It was the climax of Labour's nearly fifty year ineluctable rise, the end of the Party's 'Magnificent Journey', the start of 'Their Great Adventure', one more step 'Out of Bondage'.[8]

Just as Socialism was seen to be the culmination of long-term economic processes so the Labour Party was thought to stand at the apex of inexorable political developments. To John Parker of the Fabians, the Party represented 'the latest attempt of the forces of the Left to extend the rights of common people against the forces of privilege'. It was 'the inheritor of the achievements of those who fought for liberty in the past', the contemporary expression of an English radical tradition which stretched back to the Peasants' Revolt.[9] Consistent with this historical viewpoint was the party's emphasis on its classless character. The 1945 victory was due, not just to working-class support, but also the votes of 'men and women of goodwill among all classes.' Labour was, as it continually reiterated throughout the 1940s, the 'People's Party'.[10] The 'People', in the first instance, were defined economically as that nine-tenths of the population forced to work for a living. In other words, Labour was the party of 'the producers, the consumers, the useful people.'[11] The contrast with the Conservatives was dramatic. Labour's General Secretary Morgan Phillips described his party's MPs as 'your own men and women, who stand with you in the workshops and factories, the offices, the fields, and men and women of attainment in professional spheres'. He went on to characterise the Conservatives as 'the big landowners, the captains of industry, the financial magnates, the powerful merchants, the cartel controllers, the bankers, the landlords and the rentiers'.[12] The main division within the electorate was between the vast majority of 'productive workers' who voted Labour and the tiny minority of 'non-productive workers'.[13]

Labour had inherited the term 'the People' from nineteenth century radicalism. The concept had been given a new vitality during the war by Labour-inclined progressives such as J.B. Priestley and Richard Acland. It was particularly attractive to Labour because it united ideological belief and electoral advantage with economic necessity. It underlined the Party's claim that Socialism, being a more efficient form of production, would properly utilise the skills of those managers, technicians and white collar workers whose votes were required if it were to win power. Before the 1945 general election, Herbert Morrison talked of the need to free British industry from the burden of the 'privileged, uncreative ... amiable, useless, part-time, old school-tie, aristocratic or MP nominee director' who treated his post as a sinecure. Under Labour efficient, salaried management – in whose hands technical skill was concentrated – would be free to pursue a more productive working partnership with the rest of the labour force.[14]

A Socialist People

Although described largely in socio-economic terms, the 'People' were not thought to have turned to the Party purely out of material self-interest. Labour denied that its brand of Socialism was exclusively materialist. The Party was also an agency for individual moral improvement, the pre-requisite of which was, admittedly, material plenty. In 1940 Attlee had told a BBC radio audience:

> The Labour Party owes its inspiration not to some economic doctrine or some theory of class domination. It has always based its propaganda on ethical principles. We believe that every individual should be afforded the fullest opportunity for developing his or her personality.[15]

19

The 'People' were those who had seen the necessity of this. Even Conservative voters, decent folk who had unfortunately been misled about the facts, would eventually see the error of their ways.[16]

The Party's relationship with the electorate was generally thought to be unproblematic. It was widely assumed that Labour was the 'representative' force which would 'lead' a willing populace into a better world.[17] Labour members were simply those who had more completely attained the appropriate form of consciousness. Members, drawn from every class, had joined a fellowship in which time and energy were freely expended to further the interests of the cause. This 'anonymous selfless service is the reality of Socialism and the guarantee that it would work.'[18] Those who remained outside were encouraged to join: the aim of at least one membership campaign was to enrol every Labour voter.[19] However, it was assumed that given time most people would enter the Party, so little else was done to break down the barriers between Party and people. In 1946 the National Executive Committee (NEC) discussed establishing a national network of bookshops which would sell Labour and progressive literature in the hope they would form 'centres of literary culture and knowledge.'[20] Stephen Taylor, Morrison's Parliamentary Private Secretary, hoped that after the 1950 General Election branches in safe seats would invite the public to attend selection meetings and take their views into consideration.[21] However, most comments on the subject began and ended with calls for more and better propaganda. No Party conference was complete without at least one delegate calling for the 'old evangelical spirit', for the Party 'to go back to the street corner where we came from, to go back to the doorstep, to the factory gate, and to express what is truly within us.'[22] The majority remained confident that Labour's message was sound and that, eventually, all reasonable people would agree with it.

Although 1945 was thought to have inaugurated a period of transition between capitalism and Socialism it was never stated how protracted this stage would be. Michael Young of the Labour Party's Research Department was unusual in specifying 1960 as a date by which the socialist society might have been built.[23] The transition was, by necessity, to be prolonged because Labour wanted to achieve Socialism through existing constitutional means. Stalin's forced march was not to be emulated.[24] Labour was implementing 'planning with freedom', charting an unknown middle course between the extremes of the United States and Soviet Union.[25]

Furthermore Labour's form of Socialism would not come overnight because it was conceived as the product of both structural reform and individual change. Whereas it was possible for the former to be quickly legislated, the latter could not. Although 1945 was seen as the product of a new mood within the electorate, even most Labour voters were still felt to have fallen some way short of a definitely socialist outlook. The party had to show the people that, as Barbara Castle put it, 'our task is something bigger than just ending queues and raising pensions and wages.'[26] It was appreciated that this would not be easy: to become a Socialist entailed a fundamental transformation in an individual's values. The nature of this change was outlined by the Labour chair of Plymouth's Housing Committee. He was confident that tenants would be able to afford increased rents which better council housing entailed, because they would save money by willingly turning their backs on an old way of life.

> It means they must go without some things – they can't go greyhound racing or do the pools or smoke twenty cigarettes a day or buy monster comics … *We're building a new race of people who won't want to do those things.* You must see it. They won't want amusements made for them. They'll make their own amusements in the community centres, in the schools with their children. They'll come home from work and dig in their gardens. You see. Fresh cabbages from the garden, instead of paying a shilling in the shops. Fresh beans

and peas. Think of that for the children. And flowers. Think
of the flowers. You see. They can pay, they will pay, if you
give them something worth paying for. We've had to take
risks, giving houses to people who need them rather than
those who can pay for them, but we've only had to turn three
people out for not paying their rent ... And you see the
children. You must look at the children.[27]

The emphasis on individual moral improvement did not
stand on its own. Democratic Socialism required the creation
of material conditions which could only come from increased
productivity.[28] Initially, Labour relied on the willingness of
workers themselves to increase output. In fact, without the
'hard work' of the producers the building of Socialism was
not possible.[29] In the period of transition, it was the 'useful
people' who would be responsible for the improved material
conditions which would form the basis upon which their
moral transformation would be completed.[30] As one stalwart
wrote, 'When men and women have won their bread, built
their houses and made life fundamentally secure, the finer
work can begin.'[31]

Enhanced morality and the achievement of higher levels of
material wealth were seen as connected in a dialectical way. It
was thought that a fairer distribution of the 'national cake'
would encourage workers to increase productivity, thereby
further expanding the size of the cake.[32] G.D.H. Cole
predicted that, 'In the long run, the strongest persuasion will
perhaps come from the spreading realisation that upon high
production depends the standard of living of the whole
people ...'[33] Production would increase once workers realised
that the fruits of their labour would be distributed amongst
the people as whole rather than find its way into the pockets
of undeserving shareholders. Work would be infused not by
individual greed but by an increasing desire for public
service.[34]

Economic Reality

Unfortunately, the Government's economic difficulties multiplied after 1945. The abrupt termination of 'Lend-Lease' and the appalling winter of 1947 merely compounded the problem of converting a wartime economy to peacetime needs. It was soon appreciated that not all the economic preconditions for Socialism were present. Pre-war rhetoric had emphasised that capitalism had solved the problem of production, Labour merely had to solve the problem of distribution. Socialism was seen as simply a matter of controlling those powers unleashed by capitalism.[35] However, soon after taking office, Labour was faced with the dual task of building Socialism whilst also saving capitalism.[36] In 1947 Morrison announced that:

> In Britain today the battle of Socialism is the battle for production. Anything that delays or lessens production is a blow in the face for the organised workers and their cause. Today any avoidable strike – whether caused by employers or workers – is sabotage; and an unofficial strike is sabotage with violence to the body of the Labour Movement itself.[37]

Although a year later Morrison came to describe production as 'the bridge to socialism' by that time it had almost become an end in itself.

Therefore, the transitional period between capitalism and Socialism was one of continued and even increased scarcity. Government had to allocate resources as best it could on behalf of the greater good. In the unique circumstances of peacetime full employment, workers were required to work harder than they had ever done before without the capitalist disciplines of poverty or the sack.[38] An increasing number feared that the moral-material dialectic was emerging too slowly. By 1949 Fabians were being warned that, 'If we cannot generate a greater respect for the common good, productivity may fall, our social schemes may fail and our living standards decline.'[39] It was evident that the transition

23

from capitalism to Socialism would be even more prolonged, complicated and confusing than had at first been thought. Needing the transformation of a whole culture, Socialism was confronted by dilatory attitudes in which the acquisitive spirit stubbornly remained central.[40]

It is in this light that Morrison's call in 1948 for the 'consolidation' of Labour's reform programme should be interpreted. By nationalising key industries, creating the National Health Service and establishing full employment Labour, Morrison said, had constructed the institutional framework from which Socialism could emerge. The time had come to test whether the, 'ideals and purposes which were enshrined in legislation are to become a living reality, or whether human imperfections will convert the dream of the reformers into just another bit of bureaucratic routine.' It was 'now the citizen's task to match the new legislation with a new spirit and a new effort.'[41] Some months later Richard Crossman, of the 'Keep Left' group of MPs, wrote that the Labour government had 'nearly all the powers it requires for building a socialist society' but 'had only legislated Socialism; during the next five years the people must begin to live it'. Instead of further extending the boundaries of the state sector there would – and should – be, 'a much more rapid advance towards Socialism in everyday life'.[42]

The Dream Fades

In spite of Morrison's intentions, 'consolidation' did not act as an opportunity for Labour to gather breath on the road to Socialism. It marked the end of the journey. Yet, after the Party's defeat in the 1951 General Election this was not immediately apparent. In that campaign Labour had won even more votes than in 1945 – some 200,000 more than the victorious Conservatives. In the same year individual party membership reached an unprecedented 876,275. Morgan Phillips, informed the NEC that the party had won a 'Victory in votes' concluding, 'we can be confident that final victory for democratic socialism is assured.'[43]

Despite surviving the electoral reverses of the 1930s, confidence in the inevitability of Socialism was not sustained with the same degree of assurance during the thirteen years of Conservative rule which followed 1951. This was not just because the 1950s contained two further electoral defeats, a decreasing popular vote and fall in Party membership: Labour never reached the depths of 1931. The situation appeared far worse because capitalism was providing more and more voters with an ever-growing array of consumer goods. Unemployment remained at a remarkably low level whilst the Conservatives were committed to maintaining the Welfare State. This was not supposed to happen. Even before 1951, Labour revisionists of both the left and right felt that they had entered a country which, according to their firmest precepts, could not exist. It seemed that Labour had created a hybrid economic system which, while it remained free of mass unemployment and poverty remained some considerable distance from Socialism.[44] By the end of the 1950s many voters even began to consider the Conservatives to be the 'modern' party. In contrast, having been left behind by history, Labour appeared 'old-fashioned'.[45]

Despite the palpable failure of 'lived Socialism' to emerge after 'consolidation' many in the party clung to the vision which had comforted them in the years before 1939. Morrison, in particular, refused to question his view of the world, blaming the electorate for not living up to Labour's expectations. 'The creditable public spirit of millions', he wrote in 1960, had 'weakened under the stress of day-to-day living' after 1945. The idealism and 'fine moral spirit' so evident during the war had not been strong enough to become the basis for Socialism.[46] Labour had led but the people proved themselves too weak to follow. Bitterness and recrimination were responses to popular fallibility. However, perhaps most simply despaired, asking themselves the question that was to haunt the Party during the following four decades: 'what went wrong?'

Notes

[1] H. Morrison, 'Considerations arising out of the general election 1951', National Executive Committee Minutes (hereafter NECM), 12 December 1951. This chapter is a shortened version of my 'Labourism in the 1940s', *Twentieth Century British History*, Volume 3, 1992.

[2] 'Socialism, RIP', *Sunday Times*, 12 April 1992.

[3] C.R. Attlee, *The Labour Party in Perspective*, Gollancz, London 1937, pp15, 281-4 and 277-9.

[4] G.D.H. Cole, 'The War on the Home Front', *Fabian Tracts*, Number 247, 1940, pp5-6 and 'Mr. Attlee's call – "I want the party to be ready!" ', NECM, February 1944.

[5] M. Young, *Labour's Plan for Plenty*, Gollancz, London 1947, p9.

[6] *Labour Party Year Book*, London 1946, pvi.

[7] *Daily Herald*, 3 November 1945.

[8] The respective titles of a contemporary book, film and play all of which celebrated the achievements of the Labour Movement.

[9] J. Parker, *Labour Marches On*, Penguin, Harmondsworth 1947, pp 13-15 and Attlee, *op.cit.*, p22.

[10] F. Williams, *Fifty Years March*, Odhams, London 1951, pp358-9.

[11] H. Morrison, *The Peaceful Revolution*, Allen and Unwin, London 1949, p47.

[12] *Labour Party Pamphlets and Leaflets* (hereafter *LPPL*), Harvester, Brighton 1981, 1945/32.

[13] *Labour Woman*, April 1950.

[14] *Daily Herald*, 30 April 1945.

[15] C.R. Attlee, *War Comes to Britain*, Gollancz, London 1940, p253 and *Labour Woman*, January 1950.

[16] *LPPL*, 1950/37.

[17] For example, see S. Cripps, *Democracy Alive*, Sidgwick and Jackson, London 1946, p30, 37.

[18] M.A. Hamilton, *The Labour Party Today*, Labour Book Service, London 1939, p94; Young, *op.cit.*, p9 and *LPPL*, 1944/5.

[19] *LPPL*, 1945/22.

[20] *Labour Party Conference Annual Report* (hereafter *LPCAR*) 1946, p116.

[21] S. Taylor, 'Socialism and Public Opinion' in D. Munro (ed), *Socialism. The British Way*, Essential Books, London 1948, pp229-30.

[22] *LPCAR* 1949, pp115-17.

[23] Young, *op.cit.*, p11.

[24] A.E. Lindsay, 'The philosophy of the British Labour government' in F.S.C. Northrop (ed), *Ideological Differences and World Order*, Yale University Press, New Haven 1949, pp250-1 and Young, *op.cit.*, pp10-11.

[25] For an exposition on this theme, see B. Wootton, *Freedom under Planning*, Allen and Unwin, London 1945.

[26] *Labour Woman*, September 1945 and January 1946.

[27] L. Thompson, *Portrait of England: News From Somewhere*, Gollancz,

London 1952, pp19-20. Emphasis added.
[28] *Daily Herald*, 23 October 1944.
[29] C.R. Attlee, *Purpose and Policy*, Hutchinson, London 1947, p79; Cripps, *Democracy, op cit*. p63 and *Daily Herald*, 26 February 1945.
[30] J. Strachey, *Why You Should be a Socialist*, Gollancz, London 1944, p77.
[31] *Labour Organiser*, July, 1949.
[32] H.A. Marquand, 'Our Production Plan' in Fabian Society, *Forward From Victory*, Gollancz, London 1946, pp53-4.
[33] G.D.H. Cole, 'The Socialisation Programme for Industry' in Munro, *op.cit.*, p47.
[34] Young, *op.cit.*, pp19 and 48.
[35] Strachey, *op.cit.*, p67.
[36] Morrison, *op.cit.*, pp47-8.
[37] *Ibid.*, p38, 34-5.
[38] *Daily Herald*, 20 August 1945.
[39] *Fabian News*, March 1949.
[40] N. Barou, 'Conclusion' in N. Barou (ed), *The Co-operative Movement in Labour Britain*, Gollancz, London 1948, p135 and Cole, 'Socialisation Programme', *op cit.*, p49.
[41] Morrison, *Peaceful Revolution, op cit.*, pp45-6.
[42] *New Statesman*, 27 November 1948.
[43] NECM, 7 November 1951.
[44] See essays by R.H.S. Crossman and C.A.R. Crosland in R.H.S. Crossman (ed), *New Fabian Essays*, Dent, London 1970 edn.
[45] For example, see M. Abrams and R. Rose, *Must Labour Lose?*, Penguin, Harmondsworth 1960.
[46] H. Morrison, *An Autobiography*, Odhams, London 1960, pp284-6.

A Golden Past?: The Labour Party and the Working Class in 1945

Robert Looker

> ... many socialists ... have come to accept the notion of socialist decline, of the past as militant and committed, and the present as unregenerate.
>
> Ralph Miliband, *Socialism and the Myth of the Golden Past*, 1964[1]

Faced with times as clearly unregenerate as our own, it is very tempting for socialists to search the past for some more heroic time of socialist struggle. As Labour politicians abandon even the rhetoric of 'Socialism' and 'class'; as the electoral ties between class and party attenuate; as the trade unions sink into post 'new realist' timidity – many on the Left now look back nostalgically to the immediate post-war period as a time when the working class, Socialism and 'the Labour Movement' seemed bound up in a common enterprise.[2]

The following discussion seeks to identify some of the important dimensions of the class-party relationship underlying the often ambiguous rhetoric of 'the Labour Movement' and the ways in which they worked in the years around 1945. Its aim is to throw some light on the view that 1945 constituted a highpoint in Labour Party-working-class relations in Britain.

28

Traditionally, the Labour Party has been characterised as 'the party of the working class'. Yet the assumptions underpinning this assertion are rarely spelt out and often contradictory images and aspirations are mobilised behind such phrases by party leaders, rank and file activists, trade union bosses and ordinary working-class voters. However, academic proponents of such claims usually direct attention to five core components of the relationship. They posit a core *electoral* connection between the Labour Party and the working class which is underpinned by a complex set of shared *identities* and common *interests*. These are in turn secured by a range of *institutional* linkages in the work place and the community. Finally, Labour faces no effective *alternative* for its role as the authentic political expression of the British working class. I shall examine each in turn.

The Electoral Connection

Historically, the politics of Labourism have centred on electoralism, and its relationship with the working class has been framed by this. The party represented the class politically in and through the electoral process. However this produced a core tension at the heart of Labour ideology and practice. On the one hand, it was organised for and dedicated to the task of winning votes at elections. On the other, it saw itself not as a 'mere electoral machine' but as the political wing of a wider 'Labour Movement', embracing labour organisations – centrally trade unions – and the wider working class. This tension has been one source of continuing conflict within Labour politics. It has turned, not on the extent of the commitment to electoralism – as Miliband has shown that has always been central to the ideology and practice of Labourism[3] – but over how far the class orientation should constrain Labour's appeal to the electorate as a whole.

In this respect, the electoral landslide of 1945[4] – along with

29

the results in 1950 and 1951 – seemed to go a long way to resolving these tensions. In 1945, Labour not only secured the largest share of the popular vote – 48.3 per cent to the Conservatives 39.8 per cent – but also won a majority of support from all age groups and from both men and women.[5] And while it received a quarter of middle-class votes, it also decisively won the support of a clear majority of the entire working class.

In the previous election in 1935, Labour had been confined to its traditional bases among organised workers in areas dominated by old heavy industry – northern towns in the main – and to areas of concentrated poverty such as east and south London. 1945, by contrast, saw the Party dramatically expand its working class base beyond this 'old working class' to embrace large swathes of workers in the new manufacturing and service industries in the Midlands and East Anglia.[6] For perhaps the first time in its history, Labour could legitimately boast that its electoral appeal encompassed all sections of the working class.[7] 1945 was Labour's 'great leap forward' as far as its electoral anchorage in the working class was concerned. Consolidated further in the 1950 and 1951 elections, this pattern was not seriously challenged until the late 1970s. It achieved this, moreover, with a programme which claimed directly to address working class identities and interests.

Class Identities

Labour's success in 1945 was dependent on it securing the support of the mass of the working class. A major element in achieving this rested on a widespread sense of identification by workers with Labour precisely because it was seen by them as 'our party'. After all, the party in the 1940s was visibly a product of and steeped in working class experience, albeit drawn disproportionately from one side of the sexual division of labour within the class. Its mass membership was predominantly, though by no means exclusively, working class.[8] Its parliamentary representatives included a sizeable number of MPs of manual working-class origins[9] as did key figures in the cabinet, including Bevin, Bevan and Shinwell. Such ties of shared social origins grounded a corresponding set of identities binding MPs and Labour leadership to their working-class voters and fostered a sense on both sides of their being 'our people'. It was a time when Labour was not afraid to talk the language of class.

However, this picture of shared identities binding party and class together needs qualification at several levels. For one thing, such class identities were ambiguous and misleading. For many working-class MPs, involvement in Labour and parliamentary politics was a mechanism for social mobility out of the class. Moreover, the shared identity was frequently imbued with a paternalist assumption that the MPs possessed a 'natural right' to speak on behalf of 'the lads' and that their views reflected the latter's best interests. In practice, the proclaimed identity involved as much calculation as concern about what workers wanted or would tolerate when it came – as it often did while Labour was in office – to calling for sacrifices. Opposition from workers, in the form of strikes and demonstrations was either dismissed or attacked as the work of 'outside agitators', as in the London dock strike of 1949.[10]

Moreover, at a time when the manual/non-manual divide was central to class identity in Britain, a majority of MPs and Cabinet members – Stafford Cripps, Hugh Dalton and Clement Attlee among them – were from middle-class backgrounds and a rising number of parliamentary 'young Turks' such as Hugh Gaitskell, Harold Wilson, Richard Crossman and Anthony Crosland were recruited from academe rather than from the unions. Differences in social background were not themselves crucial in determining political leanings, but they served to reinforce the ideological divisions between right and left in the party. Right-wing trade unionists distrusted much left-wing rhetoric not least because it came from middle-class 'intellectuals', while working-class left-wingers saw middle-class 'revisionists' as doubly suspect.

More significantly, Labour's identification with the working class was never unequivocal, reflecting not only its sense of electoral realities but also its ideological self-definition as a 'national' rather than a 'class' party – the latter was an accusation to be thrown at the Tories. Indeed, a case can be made for seeing Labour's victory in 1945 as a triumph more for its 'national' than its 'class' identity. Certainly, there was a powerful spirit of national unity permeating wartime Britain which was underpinned by feelings and experiences of solidarity and sacrifice in a shared struggle. Yet underlying this there was a strong class divide in the aspirations to which such sentiments gave rise. For large sections of the working class, whether in uniform or in the workplace, the collectivist and egalitarian impulses of wartime Britain underlined the necessity of making a break from the miseries and oppressions of the pre-war system. And while Mass Observation found that only a tiny minority of the population expected or hoped for revolution,[11] the war radicalised popular expectations about the future to a degree that only fundamental changes in the post-war social order could hope to satisfy; and for a majority of them, only a Labour victory could bring them about.[12] Perhaps the class nature of the 1945 election victory is best testified to by the contrast between the celebrations of working people of 'their' victory and the panic which gripped many members of the ruling classes who saw the election of an 'alien' Labour government as a direct threat to their position.[13]

Class Interests

What was true for class identities was equally true for class interests. Labour, though dedicated to advancing those interests, was deeply divided ideologically as to what they were and how to accomplish this in practice. From its foundation, a core tension in Labour ideology and a central dimension of the divide between its right and left wings was over whether working-class interests were best satisfied through the protection of organised labour as a 'sectional' interest and/or by a programme of socialist transformation. Labour was also profoundly ambivalent as to how class interests related to what they saw as the wider 'national interest', whether defined in technocratic or socialist terms.[14]

1945 appeared to resolve these tensions. The policies on which Labour won the election were shaped as much by awareness of working-class felt needs as by the plans of Fabian-inspired bureaucrats and technocrats building on Labour's experience of office during the wartime coalition. In 1945 at least, what was good for the workers was also good for the nation in Labour's view. While its programmes for social welfare and economic advance had been articulated by liberal intellectuals like Beveridge and Keynes, they were at least in part a response to pressures from organised labour.[15] Moreover, their popular reception and Labour's readiness to attempt their full implementation reflected on the degradations inflicted on working-class families by poverty, ill health, bad housing and unemployment in the pre-war years. Labour thinking here was anchored in the decisive class rejection of any return to the conditions of the 1930s. 'Never again' was not simply a pious hope: it was a class demand which would brook no equivocation, as even the nervous Tories recognised.

Significantly, the nationalisation programme also provided for a while a point of convergence between Labour's rival views on class interests. When the leadership acquiesced in its inclusion in the Party programme at the 1944 Party Conference they did so in the knowledge that the measures commanded widespread support not only among conference delegates but also among workers in the industries concerned and the working-class electorate. Yet the programme's scope and mode of execution remained very much in dispute between left and right[16] and Morrisonian-style implementation soon undermined the popular appeal of nationalisation. This was as much a consequence of its limited impact on the workplace experience of workers in the nationalised industries as its disappointing overall impact on economy and society in the view of the wider electorate.[17]

In fact it was the trade union organisations, who pressed for and secured important statutory procedural and bargaining rights in the greatly expanded public sector, who were the chief beneficiaries of nationalisation within the Labour Movement. This, along with the repeal of the 1927 Trade Disputes and Trade Unions Act, and the extension of the tripartite patterns of consultation developed during wartime greatly helped to consolidate and legitimate union influence both in industry and on the wider political front.[18]

The programme on which Labour won the 1945 Election was a radical reformist one and few if any in the Labour leadership envisaged that it would bring about a socialist transformation of the capitalist social order in Britain. Nonetheless, it would be wrong to characterise working-class support for Labour in 1945 as expressing a conscious preference for reform rather than societal transformation. Such a view underestimates the widespread popular aspirations for a decisive break with an old order which had produced slump and appeasement in the pre-war period. While it was hardly a full and consciously articulated demand for a 'socialist Britain', probably a larger proportion of the working class was more receptive to such a vision in the years leading up to 1945 than at any other time in the past half century.[19]

Whatever the expectations, their translation into concrete action by the Labour government proved a somewhat mixed experience. Labour Britain between 1945-1951, both in its achievements and limitations, came to define what most workers thought Socialism was about in practice. While the mood among the mass of the working class remained sympathetic to Labour, expectations of how far such 'Socialism' could transform society were being steadily lowered. Capitalism as a system of endemic inequality and insecurity could apparently be tamed by a combination of government economic intervention, full employment and the Welfare State, albeit with a powerful and irksome admixture of bureaucratic regulation. Capitalism as a system of power and exploitation in the Marxist sense was not.

Even as a programme of 'reformist socialism', Labour found itself rapidly running out of steam. By 1947 – Dalton's *annus horrendus* – a succession of crises had reduced the Labour leadership to a state of ideological confusion and its reformist impulses to near exhaustion. By the late 1940s, any hopes of expanding the reform programme had given way to 'consolidation'. Among workers, gratitude for Labour's real if limited achievements now combined with a resigned acceptance of the present austerities of ration-book Britain rather than with hopes for a better socialist future.[20]

Institutional Ties

Underpinning the ambiguous ties of interest and identity linking Labour to the working class, there was a variegated set of organisational channels of communication between the two which collectively constituted 'the British Labour Movement'. While 'the Movement' embraced bodies such as the Co-op and the Woodcraft Folk, its most politically important lines of communication ran through the constituency parties and the affiliated trade unions. Together, they supposedly gave the party firm roots in the community and the work place while providing effective channels for political involvement and influence by workers on the Party.

How strong were these roots and how effective these channels in the 1940s? Far from building Labour's victory on a lively and vital local party structure – during the war, Party membership had in fact declined under the combined impact of mobilisation and the 'party truce' pursued during the wartime coalition – victory in 1945 was itself the stimulus for expansion. Both party membership and activity at the grass roots grew rapidly in the late 1940s and peaked in 1952. However, party life in the Constituency Labour Parties (CLPs) even at this highpoint in the 1940s revealed that Labour's 'grass roots' were pretty shallow in working-class communities; the constituency parties were limited in their size of membership and levels of activity, and were usually more concerned with administrative matters and social life than with political involvement and debate.[21]

In Britain, active participation in politics for workers was always more a matter of involvement in the trade unions rather than constituency organisations. However the 'union voices' that Labour leaderships heard and listened to were at best only indirectly those of the rank and file. Though formally democratic, union structures were often in practice both oligarchic and bureaucratic. For the most part, it was the predominantly right-wing union leaders of the 'big six' – among them Arthur Deakin of the TGWU, Will Lawther of the NUM and Tom Williamson of the NUGMW – who wielded real influence in the 1940s[22]. At their most expansive, they could act as spokesmen not only for their individual unions but also for organised labour as a whole. However, their views were usually framed by right-wing perspectives and often put their own organisational interests above those of their own rank and file membership, not to mention those of the wider working class. As the historic creators and continuing paymasters of the Labour Party, they expected their views to be given some weight by a Labour government, particularly on the industrial front. The relationship was lubricated by a combination of informal consultation between the two leaderships and more formal control of union bloc votes which could be used to support, embarrass or even challenge party leadership and policy where necessary.[23]

For its part, the Labour leadership saw the union connection as a mixed blessing. They welcomed its financial and electoral support but were profoundly uneasy in the face of opposition taunts that they were 'tools of the unions'. One touchstone of their status as a 'responsible' and 'national' government required Labour periodically to 'stand up to the unions'. At the same time they needed their close ties with the unions and the latter's sense of loyalty to 'our government' to cajole and, if necessary, threaten them into supporting policies which were disliked or opposed by organised labour. Crucially, between 1948 and 1950, Labour relied on its links with the union leaderships to secure both their reluctant acquiescence to pay restraint and productivity policies and to enlist them in imposing discipline on a restive rank and file.[24]

From the Coalition government in 1940 through to 1951, Labour in office was periodically confronted by industrial strikes and other forms of militant class action, often in direct response to government pressures and policies. From the wartime disputes in the mines through to the rash of strikes from 1947 onwards, Labour proved ready to deploy the coercive agencies of the state – police, army, courts – against them.[25] In office, Labour was committed to the view that in any clash between 'the Labour Movement' and the State, it was the former that must give way.

Challenges and Alternatives

Labour's claim to be the sole and authentic 'party of the working class' was never unchallenged. Throughout its history, rival left parties have sought either to dispute Labour's electoral hegemony or to construct a different kind of class politics around industrial and extra-parliamentary class struggles. In the 1940s, the most important external competitor was the Communist Party[26] but its influence was hostage to the fortunes of the popularity or otherwise of the Soviet Union. Thus while it benefitted from popular support for the post-1941 Soviet alliance against Hitler, the onset of the Cold War from 1947 and the Communist Party's near total pre-occupation with 'American Imperialism' marginalised its influence among the mass of workers who were either uninterested in foreign policy or hostile to the USSR.

Other challenges to the dominant Labourist tradition came from within the party, particularly but not exclusively from the Left.[27] However, the Labour Left, from 'Keep Left' to the 'Bevanites', conducted its opposition almost entirely within the framework of Labour institutions, in parliamentary caucuses or through conference resolutions and debates. Unfortunately, the legitimating basis for this strategy – its claim to 'speak on behalf of the Labour Movement' – lacked real organisational and sociological content. While it could embarrass and even occasionally defeat the leadership on particular issues, it was never remotely likely to transform the theory and practice of Labourism. Rather, it was the 'revisionist' and 'modernising' Right which succeeded in re-shaping Labour policy in the decades after 1951.

A Golden Age?

In heeding warnings against some myth of golden past, we need to avoid the alternative 'myth of an ever grey present' which ignores the historical variability in the relationships between the Labour Party and the working class. A case can be made for treating 1945-51 as the highpoint of this relationship and portraying 1945 as the apogee of a certain vision of class politics – of a working class that assumed that the Labour Party was 'our party' and would represent our interests. If those interests required the establishment of a socialist order, so be it. In 1945, the British working class as a whole came as near as it has done in this century to will that end. In the event, they settled for a lot less. It is also possible to argue that in 1945 the socialist rhetoric of the 'Labour Movement' – an intertwining of industrial and political wings united in a programme of fundamental change in society – came closer to reality than it has ever done in its history.

The achievements that the 1945-51 Labour governments effected for the working class were real but limited. While they had a generally beneficial impact on the lives of most working people, they never set out to address, still less to confront, the fundamental facts of class power and class exploitation in capitalism. Rather they tried to distance and insulate significant areas of working class life – health, education, social security, housing – from the logic and imperatives of capital and of the market. The results were inherently contradictory: a paternalistic welfare state subjected to tight bureaucratic control, whose universalistic aspirations were limited in practice by tight funding; an interventionist State committed to full employment, economic growth and improved living standards, social justice and a nationalised sector – but only to the extent that this was compatible with profitability and accumulation in the capitalist economy as a whole. Improvements in welfare such as family allowances pre-supposed rather than challenged the prevailing sexual division of labour. Limited advances in trade union bargaining rights and access to government depended on the unions exercising these with 'restraint' and 'responsibility'. Overall, the Labour government advanced working-class needs and interests, but only insofar as these were firmly specified as one more sectional interest among the many competing for relative advantage within a capitalist social order.

So even at its apogee, the party-class 'compact of 1945' proved flawed and limited in its capacity either to deliver Socialism by instalments or to advance and entrench the sectional interests of workers securely. If 1945-1951 was the high tide in the relationship between the Labour Party and the working class, it was also – to mix metaphors – an historical watershed. The rhetoric of 'the Labour Movement' concealed core weaknesses, ambiguities, tensions and contradictions, which the experience of the first majority Labour government was bound to expose to view. Faced with the test of practice of 1945-1951, the classical Labourist rhetoric of 'the Labour Movement' – of a party and a class united in a programme for socialist advance – could survive only as a nostalgic myth.

Notes

[1] Ralph Miliband, 'Socialism and the myth of the Golden Past' in R. Miliband & J. Saville (eds), *The Socialist Register*, Merlin Press, London 1864, p92.

[2] The left's nostalgia for the 1940s was powerfully influenced if not originated by Eric Hobsbawm's 'forward march' thesis in the late 1970s and the debates it sparked off. See E. Hobsbawm *et al*, *The Forward March of Labour Halted*, Verso, London 1981, and note in particular Tony Benn's contribution on pp78-80. For a powerful manifestation of the 'unregenerate times' view, see James Hinton, *Labour and Socialism*, Wheatsheaf, Brighton 1983, chapter 11. In Hinton's view, by the 1980s, 'the labour movement no longer had the capacity to resist' Thatcherism because 'what had disintegrated ... was precisely the sense of a movement – the sense that each local and particular struggle, and each part of the institutional structure, was in some way linked to the whole by a common socialist purpose, a commitment, however vague and ambiguous, to the construction of a new social order'. (pp197-8).

[3] R. Miliband, *Parliamentary Socialism*, Allen and Unwin, London 1961.

[4] With a 12 per cent swing from Conservative to Labour, it involved the biggest movement in votes in an election since 1918. See David Butler, *British General Elections since 1945*, Blackwell, Oxford 1989, p9.

[5] See Henry Durant, 'Voting Behaviour in Britain 1945-1966', in Richard Rose (ed), *Studies in British Politics*, (2nd ed.) Macmillan, London 1969, particularly pp168-169.

[6] One indicator of this is provided by the differential swings to Labour in cities such as Glasgow – only 2½ per cent – and Birmingham – 23 per cent. See R.B. McCallum & A. Readman, *The British General Election of 1945*, Oxford University Press, Oxford 1947, especially Chapter XIV and Appendix IV.

[7] However some 40 per cent of manual workers voted for other parties in 1945 – see Butler *ibid*, p62.

[8] See Tom Forester, *The Labour Party and the Working Class*, Heinemann, London 1976, pp86-93. For more recent data see Patrick Seyd & Paul Whiteley, *Labour's Grass Roots*, Oxford University Press, Oxford 1992.

[9] For the changing composition of the PLP see W.L. Guttsman, *The British Political Elite*, MacGibbon & Kee, London 1964, particularly pp272-273.

[10] See P. Weiler, 'British Labour and the Cold War: The London Dock Strike of 1949', in J.E. Cronin & J. Schneer (eds), *Social Conflict and the Political Order in Modern Britain*, Croom Helm, Beckenham 1982.

[11] Cited by Peter Hennessy, *Never Again*, Jonathan Cape, London 1992, p79.

[12] For a discussion of the popular mood in the war-time years prior to the 1945 election see Angus Calder, *The People's War*, Jonathan Cape, London 1969 and Paul Addison, *The Road to 1945*, Jonathan Cape, London 1975.

[13] See Hennessy, *op. cit.*, p88 and Anthony Howard, 'We are the Masters Now' and David Pryce-Jones, 'Towards the Cocktail Party' in Michael Sissons & Philip French (eds), *Age of Austerity 1945-51*, Penguin, Hardmondsworth 1964.

[14] Ramsay McDonald's 1905 volume on *Socialism and Society* is frequently cited as one of the earliest and clearest statements of the elevation of 'national' over 'class' interests in the specification of Socialism.

[15] As Calder points out, 'the first impetus for the Beveridge report had come from the TUC', *op.cit*, p525.

[16] The case for industrial democracy won significant backing from the unions in the 1930s – see David Coates, *The Labour Party and the Struggle for Socialism*, Cambridge University Press, London 1975, pp35-37. See also Richard Saville, 'Commanding Heights', in Jim Fyrth (ed), *Labour's High Noon: The Government and the Economy*, Lawrence and Wishart, London 1993.

[17] D. Coates, *op.cit*, p47-54.

[18] See A. Calder, *op.cit.*, pp383-400.

[19] Though the strength of such sentiments shouldn't be underestimated either: see for instance the report that as early as 1942, Mass Observation surveys 'showed a general belief that some sort of socialism was inevitable'. Socialism in this context was not simply equated with Labour; indeed in 1942, such sentiments were 'coupled with a very frequent disillusion in the Labour Party and Socialist leaders'! See Tom Harrisson, 'Who'll win? 1944, p215 in A. Calder & D. Sheridan (eds), *Speak for Yourself*, Jonathan Cape, London 1984.

[20] Hennessy has assembled evidence for the view that the final years under Labour were as much about vitality, even fun – see Hennessy, *op.cit.*, pp306-321 – but the 'age of austerity' tag still seems the most appropriate one.

[21] T. Forester, *op.cit.*, pp78-86.

[22] The 'big six' – the TGWU, NUGMW, NUM, USDAW, NUR, AEU – controlled over half the votes at the TUC and almost half at the Labour Party Conference. See Lewis Minkin, *The Labour Party Conference*, Allen Lane, London 1978, pp23-26 and Leo Panitch, *Social Democracy and Industrial Militancy*, Cambridge University Press, Cambridge 1976, p31.

[23] For the classic statement of the role of the union bosses as the 'praetorian guard' of the Labour leadership, see Robert McKenzie, *British Political Parties* (2nd ed), Heinemann, London 1963. For an extended critique see L. Minkin, 1978, *op.cit*; see also Richard Hyman, 'Praetorians and Proletarians' in J. Fyrth (ed), *op.cit.*

[24] L. Panitch, *op.cit.*, pp21-30.

[25] While the Labour government repealed the 1927 Act, it insisted in keeping wartime emergency powers regulations governing compulsory arbitration (Order 1305) in place.

[26] The Communist Party in this period is the subject of the chapter by John Callaghan below.

[27] The Labour left in this period is the subject of Jonathan Wood's chapter below.

'Daughter of the Newer Eve': The Labour Movement and Women

Christine Collette

Daughter of the Ancient Eve
We know the gifts you gave, and give;
Who knows the gifts that you shall give,
Daughter of the Newer Eve?

Quoted by Mrs K.M. Shaile, chairing
23rd National Conference of Labour Women, 1945

Although it is difficult to trace a clearly defined ideology of gender within the Labour Movement or to find direct expression of a progressive synthesis of feminism and socialism, the period of the first majority Labour government, nevertheless, represented a high point of women's experience of Labour Party and trade union participation. This efflorescence is explained by confidence gained through women's wartime experience, and led to a sustained effort to win equal pay and opportunities at work, besides laying the ground for the development of two major concerns of the 'second wave' of twentieth century feminism, peace and the provision of responsive and sensitive welfare services.

Women in the Labour Force and Labour Movement

Penny Summerfield, in her recent work on the Second World War, expresses the opinion that there was no revolution in women's status but that groups of women experienced change that was not necessarily an improvement. The proportion of older and married women in the labour force rose and this rise was sustained after the war; this was true of engineering trades (see Table One). There was much part-time work after 1945 and, despite a drift from engineering into more traditional trades, such as food, drink and tobacco, the numbers of women in, for instance, engineering, transport, local government and the Civil Service were, in 1950, double the number in 1939. The Trades Union Congress (TUC) noted in 1946, 'Employment in engineering industries has proved more attractive to these women workers than employment in the old peacetime industries'.[1]

Table One: Women in Engineering Trades, 1939 and 1946

	General Engineering	Electrical Engineering	Motor Vehicle Cycle, Aircraft	Electric Cable etc.
June, 1939	67,000	28,000	45,000	80,000
April, 1946	196,000	50,000	110,000	119,000

Source: Trades Union Congress, 78th Annual Report 1946, p167.

Even when allowances are made for inadequate records, the presence of greater numbers of women in the war-time workforce was clearly reflected in a very large growth of women in trade unions, an increase which continued, in total, after the war (Table Two). Despite a dip in the numbers of women in general labour, transport and engineering unions, the figures for 1950 were around three and seven times higher, respectively, than those of 1939, whilst women members of

Table Two: Estimate of Labour Party and Trades Union Membership, 1921-1950

	1921	1931	1939	1945	1950	
Labour Party Individual Membership[1]	N/A	N/A	168,866	195,612	364,727	Women
			239,978	291,435	543,434	Men
Trade Union Membership[2]	1,033,00	763,000	975,538	1,638,000	1,670,000	Women
	5,760,000	3,848,000	5,258,018	6,237,000	7,565,000	Men
General Labour and Transport			84,025	292,210	278,950*	Women
	1,143,113*	811,000	1,384,886	1,407,230	1,500,360	Men Combined
Metals Machines Engineering			8,587	98,420	56,900	Women
	978,908	563,000	927,538	1,384,830	1,591,480	Men Combined
Clerical, Public Service & Local Government			49,649††	78,830††	105,750††	Women
			183,959	202,170	269,260	Men
	196,888†	372,000**				Combined

Sources: [1] 50th Annual Conference of the Labour Party, *Report*, 1951, p36.
[2] Board of Trade & Ministry of Labour *Gazette*. The estimates of total trades union membership given at the end of the current year sometimes varied in retrospect. Individual unions were grouped differently in different years, so comparisons are not easy to make. The figures should, therefore, be treated with caution; however, the trends in membership are obvious.

Key: * General Labour only.
† public administration.
** including national government.
†† local government.

local government unions had nearly doubled in number. The Labour Party was able to capitalise on this to win recruits so that women's war-time experience contributed to the vitality of both the industrial and political wings of the Labour Movement after 1945.[2] Representing women of the working classes, female Labour Movement activists had no problem in identifying women both as wage earners and people who consciously sought improved living and working conditions. For instance, Dame Anne Loughlin told the 1951 Labour Party Conference, 'When I hear people talk about the trade unions and the Labour Party as if they were something separate it leaves me a little puzzled because to me the movement is indivisible'. Similarly, Florence Davy, looking back on a lifetime of Labour Movement activity, that included organising for the Union of Post Office Workers and serving on Hackney Council during the war wrote, 'Unity of the Labour Party, Trade Union Movement and Co-operative Movement is essential to success.'[3]

Moreover, some few of these women had experience of Communist Party activity. As the drop in individual membership of the Labour Party illustrated (Table Two), constituencies were disrupted by the war, by bombing raids which kept activists at home, the conscription of agents and evacuation.[4] One of the results was that political consciousness was developed not in the locality, where the Labour Party operated but in the workplace, where the Communist Party was most active.[5] By 1942 Communist Party membership was one quarter that of the Labour Party. The story told by Annie Leff was familiar: recruited from the furnishing trade to manufacture wooden aircraft, she became active in her union and joined the Communist Party. Therein, she claimed she experienced neither gender discrimination nor anti-semitism, enjoyed political discussion and admired administrative expertise (all in contrast to her experience of the Labour Party, which she joined in 1956).[6] Like Annie Leff, some Communist recruits remained in membership, at least until 1956. Others joined the Labour Party when

Communist fortunes fell after 1945; such women could hardly be considered politically ignorant of either class or gender politics.

Women interviewed for Labour Heritage, an association aiming to inspire interest in and preserve the records of Labour Party history, have recorded intense activity from 1945. For instance, Joan Davis, later Labour Group Leader of Epping Forest District Council, remembered:

> At the 1945 General Election we started to get really involved in the local Labour Party ... when you are fighting your first General Election as a newcomer to politics it is quite exciting.

Joan shortly became, at the age of twenty-two, the youngest and first woman Vice-Chair of North Kensington Labour Party. Bertha Elliott began her career as a Labour Party agent at this time, appointed from a shortlist of six, the only female candidate.[7] The growing strength of women's Labour Party membership was shown by the steady increase in Women's Sections reported by Mary Sutherland year by year; by 1947 473 had been formed; two years later the total stood at an unprecedented 1,843; followed by 297 new Sections in 1950 and 169 in 1951.[8] This growth was mirrored by an increase in Regional Women's Advisory Councils. The energy generated, spurred on by disparaging press reports which stung the women's leadership into action, led to the creation of a National Women's Advisory Council in 1951. Trade union women already had their their own National Advisory Committee.

No Ideology of Gender

Given the growth of women's Labour Party membership and their exposure during the war to Trade Union and political activity, it is a matter of some surprise that no clearer ideology of women's involvement was expressed. The unfavourable press reports indicated that Labour Party women failed to make an impact on popular opinion. The leadership's response was to increase co-ordination at the centre; the fact that the National Committee was advisory showed that there was no transfer of power, no open door for the kind of radical transformation that might have caught the popular imagination. However, regional and district women's committees did seek to reach the ordinary members by an impressive array of educational opportunities.[9] Women did not seek a separate organisation; paradoxically, their very strength and the consequent breadth of their activity may have contributed to their weakness in developing an ideology of gender. Acting as confident colleagues, rather than suffering sisters, women assumed engagement in all aspects of the Labour Party programme. The *Labour Party Conference Reports, 1945-51*, identify speakers and indicate that women addressed an eclectic range of issues. These women were, of course, extraordinary by virtue of attendance at Party Conference, but it is nevertheless interesting that they did not privilege gender issues. Only one speech on the subject of a Women's Department is recorded over the period; there were thirty-eight speeches by women on the party manifesto, thirty-five on social welfare, fourteen on the economy and thirteen on foreign affairs.

If debate at Labour Party Conference failed to elucidate an ideology of gender, so did the action of the Labour government. Continuing the opportunistic wartime treatment of women, the Government ran campaigns to recruit women to industry. That the Government forced women, *en masse*, into domesticity is not a tenable opinion. Both the TUC and the Labour Party were opposed to bars on married women's employment and the Government removed the bar for its own employees. Women were quick to spot any attempt to exclude them from employment; when in 1946 the TUC debated the abolition of female employment in the metal polishing and foundry trades, Florence Hancock of the General Council firmly stated, 'if a job is bad for women it is bad for men also'. That year the Women's Consultative

Committee, which had advised on women conscripted to industry and the armed forces was recalled 'to advise the Minister on questions relating to the resettlement of women in civilian life.'[10] There was also a recruitment drive for the Women's Land Army to compensate for the end of female conscription.[11] In 1948 the Government campaigned in districts with a shortage of female labour, successfully recruiting 14,187 women.[12] The writer Amabel Williams-Ellis, discussing for the Labour Party 'Is Women's Place in the Home?', gave the opinion that, for the first time ever, the Government of the day wanted maximum production and full employment so that there was no need for working men to fear competition from women. She took account of working people's struggle for acceptable working conditions as an understandable motive for caution about women's labour force participation, and noted fears that women would become, 'hardened, coarsened and defeminised and therefore unattractive if they work outside their homes'.[13]

Nursery Schools and Equal Pay

Having spent so much effort promoting the image of women as workers, the Government failed to follow through with measures to make the role attractive. The 100 per cent grant to local authorities for nursery provision was replaced by a block grant for welfare services, which the TUC estimated would mean halving the nursery grant. Women at the Labour Women's Conference gave greater attention to gender issues than that expressed by women at the annual Party Conference. They repeatedly asked for day nurseries and nursery schools; however, there was less support each year as women delegates expressed solidarity with a Labour government facing economic crisis.[14] The nub of the issue of women's involvement in the labour force on an equal basis to men was equal pay. It was here that women most clearly proposed a change in the ideology of gender through their

Williams-Ellis wrote, 'wage rates ... have always been determined by the relative strength of the contesting parties in the process of collective bargaining'.[19] In so far as the Labour government challenged this demarcation and presided over burgeoning women's trade unionism it did make a contribution to the equal pay campaign and to a changing ideology of gender.

Peace and Welfare

If women did not pursue their interests as workers beyond a point which would embarrass the Labour government, other issues, particularly those of peace and welfare services – traditional areas of concern for Women's Sections and Women's Co-operative Guilds – illuminated the character of women's engagement in the Labour Movement.[20] Women's impetus to international organisation had been illustrated by the launch of the International Friendship and Freedom Fund (1943), an attempt to contact socialist women in occupied countries. The revival of the Labour and Socialist International after the war gained momentum when a women's group within COMISCO (Committee of International Socialist Organisation) was formed in 1946 with Margaret Kissel of Switzerland as Secretary. Every year, resolutions were sent to Women's Conference calling for broader organisation; but, echoing the pre-war position, fear of the Soviet Union and of national Communist parties impeded progress. In 1948 Labour Party women were warned against attending International Women's Day celebrations because of communist involvement.[21] Whilst proclaiming that 'socialism, like peace, was indivisible', the women's leadership retained the right to join an appropriate (social democratic) organisation when possible rather than initiating the 'all-in' (including communist) conference for which some women called.[22]

This distancing of Labour Movement organisations from

Communism was in line with Labour government anti-communist foreign policy which led to the introduction of peacetime conscription in 1947, the formation of NATO in 1949 and the involvement in the Korean War from 1950. British forces stayed in Germany; by 1950 arms exports were double those of America;[23] the atom bomb was developed in secret under the 1946 Atomic Energy Act. Resolutions to Women's Conference, usually watered down by compositing before debate, challenged all of this programme.[24] Although Government policy always won majority support, the persistence and range of the challenge indicated substantial debate amongst Women's Sections in the constituencies. Starting a lengthy discussion at the 1948 Women's Conference, Worcester Women's Section called on Labour women to refuse to tolerate further war, and on the Government 'to keep the country strictly neutral both in word and deed should any dispute arise between the nations of the world': war led to poverty, disablement, neuroses, and broken marriages, and would spell the end of socialist services. The resolution was successfully amended to 'affirm ... loyal support of the Government's policy' in order to achieve collective action for peace, but a detailed pacifist position had been articulated.[25] In 1951 an emergency resolution from the Transport and Salaried Staff Association regretted that there was no ceasefire in Korea whilst supporting the Government, and opinions were expressed against American imperialism and the use of the atom bomb.[26]

It is always difficult to assess the extent to which the rank and file have an internationalist attitude since in this field their power is strictly limited. However, at the 1948 Women's Conference, York asked for more opportunities for rank and file international contact: 'The women of the National Executive and Members of Parliament made contact with people in other countries, but it was time that they got down to a lower level.' The difficulties here were finance and language, although Finchley's opinion was that, 'Human sympathy made a contact with which the barriers of language did not interfere.'[27] Joan Davis remembered such links in camping holidays with the League of Youth (affiliated to the International Union of Socialist Youth) which included a visit by a party of four hundred to Sweden.[28]

Domestically, local social policy offered a relatively greater chance of rank and file activity. Labour women's first great campaign, for free school meals (1906-1914) had shown that local success could be won.[29] Demands for welfare measures of a socialist nature had co-existed from the start with calls for political representation and equal rights at work, and with an international perspective. The link between peace and social services, the former a prerequisite to building economic resources for the latter, while an adequate social wage created the climate for stability, had been articulated by women at their 1948 conference. Impelled by wartime experience and by the Beveridge Report, as much as by previous experience of unemployment and poverty, the first majority Labour government made extensive welfare measures a major part of its programme. Never had conditions been so ripe for pressing women's demands on social policy. A call at Women's Conference for a Women's Ministry of Social Welfare identified this as a gender issue.[30] That social policy impacted on the ideology of gender was recognised when women campaigned for day nurseries and nursery schools.

Nevertheless, there was little evidence either of the exact nature of welfare provision sought nor its application to gender discrimination. Amabel Williams-Ellis wrote, 'Better Social Services, family allowances ... a greater recognition of the home-maker's vitally responsible work will ... also ... gradually give the woman who elects to stay at home a much greater degree of "independence" ', but did not challenge the gender of the 'homemaker'.[31] Beveridge himself envisaged a system based on the family unit, whilst the war was widely thought to have rediscovered the value of the family. Enshrined in welfare state legislation, ideas of family sited in a woman-made home failed to challenge institutionalised sexism (notoriously, in the married man's tax allowance and discriminatory national insurance contributions). In accepting this programme, women gave tacit approval to discriminatory ideology. Such a situation was by no means confined to Britain: American and Swedish historians, for instance, have drawn similar conclusions, that women felt bound to support social service provision which envisaged a domestic role for women, in default of an alternative.[32]

Party Loyalty Versus Equality

Just as child-rearing and house-keeping were allowed to remain tasks that were largely female and private, so discrimination against women workers was allowed to continue. The Labour Movement failed to make a challenge to these two twin causes of women's oppression. Women did articulate their demands, in these areas and on the issue of peace and internationalism, but chose not to embarrass the Labour government. That it was a conscious choice reflected the very active involvement of women in the Labour Movement; reasons included the desire for involvement in all aspects of the Government programme and reluctance to separate gender issues, or to give them priority over issues of class. One might see this either as a failure of gender consciousness or as a refusal of the victim role. In view of women's war-time experience, refusal of victimisation might even have been an indication of new found strength. Nevertheless, that the Labour government fell and there was no time to turn its attention specifically to discrimination against women, does not alter the case, that in the interests of Party loyalty and unity, women's strength in the Labour Movement failed to remove the main sources of women's inequality and oppression.[33]

Notes

[1] Penny Summerfield, *Women Workers in the Second World War: Production and Patriarchy in Conflict*, Routledge, London 1989, Preface and passim, pp187-8, tables on p196 and 199. Trades Union Congress, *78th Annual Report*, 1946, p167.

[2] 44th Annual Conference of the Labour Party *Report*, 1945, p10.

[3] For the development of this debate, see Mrs K.M. Shaile, 23rd Labour Women's Conference *Report*, 1945, p2; Alice Bacon, 24th Labour Women's Conference *Report*, 1946, p15; Dame Anne Loughlin, (National Union of Tailors and Garment Workers and Standing Joint Committee of Working Women's Organisations), 80th Annual Conference of the Labour Party *Report*, 1951, p176; Florence Davy, 'From Zeppelins to Jets', Labour Heritage Women's Research Committee *Bulletin* No 2, 1987. Women's refusal to separate political and industrial activity makes gender ideology resistant of definition.

[4] See James Hinton, 'Coventry Communism: A Study in Factory Politics in the Second World War', *History Workshop Journal* 10, Autumn 1980, pp90-118, cited, p94.

[5] *Ibid*, p93.

[6] Annie Leff, interview with author, 1991; work in progress, Labour Heritage Women's Research Committee *Bulletin*, Number 4.

[7] Joan Davis, 'A Life in the Labour Movement', Labour Heritage Women's Research Department *Bulletin* Number 2 1987; Bertha Elliott, amongst others, contributing to Labour Heritage Conference, 'The Influence of Women on the Formation of Socialist Thought and Politics', 18 July 1992.

[8] Annual Conference of the Labour Party *Report*, 1947, p15; 1949, p19; 1950, p21; 1951, p21.

[9] Party education was applauded at Women's Conference, see *Resolutions for Labour Party Women's Conference*, 1948, p3.

[10] Trade Union Congress, 78th Annual Report, 1946 p342-345 and pp355-356. *Labour Party Year Book 1946-47*, London 1947, p129.

[11] *Labour Party Year Book*, *op.cit.*, p16. 10,876 women were recruited.

[12] 47th Annual Conference of the Labour Party *Report*, 1948, p63.

[13] Amabel Williams-Ellis, 'Is Women's Place in the Home?', *Labour Discussion Series* Number 9, London 1947, cited, p3 and p9.

[14] Trades Union Congress, 78th Annual *Report* 1946, p168. *Resolutions*, *op.cit.*, 1946; seven resolutions submitted on nursery schools and day nurseries, pp5-6. 24th Labour Women's Conference. *Report*, 1946, pp45-46, composite resolution carried unanimously. *Resolutions op.cit.*, 1947, p3, 25th Labour Women's Conference *Report* 1947, pp32-33, resolution lost. *Resolutions op.cit.*, 1948, p6; 26th Labour Women's Conference *Report*, 1948, p38 previous questions moved. *Resolutions op.cit.*, 1946, p4; 1947, p3; 1948 p6; 1949 p10. The 1949 resolution was not referred to Women's Conference which instead debated economic policy and devaluation.

[15] 23rd Labour Women's Conference *Report*, 1945, p28. The SJCWW preferred to press for 'the rate for the job' rather than 'equal pay'; trying to establish work of equal value has bedevilled claims under the current equal pay legislation.

[16] Trade Union Congress, *77th Annual Report*, 1945, p203 and p350.

[17] Trades Union Congress, *79th Annual Report*, 1947, pp537-539; *80th Annual Report*, 1948, p465; *81st Annual Report*, 1949, pp481-482, General Council line supported 3,835,000 to 1,765,000; *82nd Annual Report*, 1950, pp454-455. Voting 4,490,000 for immediate action on equal pay, 2,367,000 against; *83rd Annual Report*, 1951, pp535-538.

[18] 48th Annual Conference of the Labour Party *Report*, 1947, pp158-159.

[19] Amabel Williams-Ellis, *op.cit.*, p4-6.

[20] See Christine Collette, *For Labour and For Women: The Women's Labour League 1906-1918*, Manchester University Press 1989, *passim* and Christine Collette, 'Women and the Labour and Socialist International' in Gabriella Hauch, *Geschlect, Klasse, Ethnizität*, Europaverlag 1993.

[21] 48th Annual Conference of the Labour Party *Report*, 1949, p6.

[22] *Resolutions, op.cit.*, 1947, p8; 1948, p3, p12. 24th Labour Women's Conference *Report*, 1946, p27; 25th Labour Women's Conference *Report*, 1947, pp27-28; 26th Labour Women's Conference *Report*, 1948, pp13-14; 'All-in' call, 27th Labour Women's Conference *Report*, 1949, p14.

[23] N. Gordon, *Conflict and Consensus in Labour's Foreign Policy 1914-1965*, Stanford 1969, p126.

[24] *Resolutions, op.cit.*, 1949, p12 against conscription; 1948, p9 and 1951, p5, against the atom bomb (neither of these reached the final agenda); 1948, p8, p9, p12, and 1951, p5 against war; 1949, p12, asking that women be included in the Government to deal with foreign affairs.

[25] 26th Labour Women's Conference *Report*, 1948, pp24-27.

[26] 28th Labour Women's Conference *Report*, 1951, pp41-44.

[27] 26th Labour Women's Conference *Report*, 1948, pp13-14.

[28] Joan Davis, *op.cit.*

[29] Christine Collette, *For Labour and For Women, op.cit. passim*. See also Patricia Hollis, *Ladies Elect: Women in Local Government 1865-1914*, Clarendon Press, Oxford 1987, *passim* for women's involvement in poor law and education reform. Amabel Williams-Ellis *op.cit.*, p13 wrote of women's interest in 'living things and social sciences'.

[30] *Resolutions, op.cit.*, 1946, p6.

[31] Amabel Williams-Ellis, *op.cit.*, p8.

[32] Susan Lynn, 'Gender and Post World War II Progressive Politics: a Bridge to Social activism in the 1960's United States of America', and Hanna Marlene Dahl, review of Yvonne Hirdman, *'Planning Life: Studies in Swedish Social Policy 1930-1950,' Gender and History* Volume 4, Number 2, Summer 1992, pp215-239.

[33] The historiography of women MPs from 1945-51 indicates clearly that their strength has been undervalued. The 1991 Ellen Wilkinson Centenary in Manchester started to reclaim a reputation suffering from accusations

made by male commentators of diminishing efficiency and influence. Labour Heritage Members, who recall the post-war years with such enthusiasm as a time of vitality, intend to arrange a suitable memorial appropriate to her distinctive career. Ellen Wilkinson 1891-1947 Centenary History Conference, National Museum of Labour History, Manchester 19 October 1991; and *see* Betty Vernon, *Ellen Wilkinson*, Croom Helm, Beckenham 1982, p123 for reference to influence on her reputation of Otto Katz/André Simone.

Wives and Citizens and Watchdogs of Equality: Post-War British Feminists

Catherine Blackford

We must discard the old idea that equality of status lies along the road of sameness ... the time has now come when we must realise that we have a contribution to human welfare which cannot be made by men.

Wife & Citizen, Journal of the
Married Women's Association, December 1948

Historical interpretations of feminism in the 1940s and 1950s have been dominated by the views of post-1960s feminists. So convinced were they that feminism had disappeared after the war, that research on women's political activity in this period did not begin until the late 1970s.[1] Although the discovery that feminism had survived challenged the prevailing view that there had been a 'political hiatus' between Women's Suffrage and Women's Liberation, feminists after the 1960s were reluctant to claim continuity with the politics of this earlier generation.[2]

They found problematic a 'feminism' which appeared to accept the primacy of marriage and motherhood in women's lives by seeking to strengthen the domestic position of women, rather than challenging the belief that the sexual division of labour in the home was either natural or desirable. Post-war feminists' methods of achieving change were also considered rather limited by Women's Liberationists. Rejecting small pressure group activity for piecemeal reform, these stressed the importance of mobilising women to act for themselves, arguing that women's liberation would result from changes in women's consciousness, rather than the law.

However, since the collapse of the Women's Liberation Movement and the fragmentation of women's political activities, some commentators have argued that it is necessary to adopt broader terms of reference when defining feminism.[3] This development in feminist theory is of particular significance for historians of women's politics, since it provides scope for a more sympathetic reading of self-identified feminism in the post-war years,[4] and the possibility of including within the history of feminism organisations and individuals who did not identify as 'feminist' themselves, but shared ideas similar to those of women who did.[5]

In this chapter however, I interpret 'feminism' narrowly to focus on those organisations which identified themselves as feminist during the post-war period, and were conscious of belonging to a feminist tradition. Although during the 1940s and 1950s the agenda of large women's organisations like the Women's Institute and the National Council of Women overlapped to some extent with that of self-identified feminism, they did not consider themselves, nor were they considered by others as feminist.[6]

Old and New Faces of Feminism

By the 1940s self-identified feminism had shrunk to a small core of London-based committees, largely backed by supporters rather than branch members. All but two were direct descendants of groups established during or just after the suffrage struggle.[7] Although one or two attracted the support of a few young women in the 1920s, and some, (the Six Point Group in particular) gained a handful of new recruits in the late 1930s, their membership was overwhelmingly composed of suffrage veterans.

The exceptions were two newer organisations: Women For Westminster and the Married Women's Association (MWA).[8] Starting life as a sub-committee of the Six Point Group, the leadership of the MWA believed that it would be able to develop and expand its work among married women only if it maintained a distance from older feminists. It decided not to use the term 'feminist' in its literature for fear this might deter support from women in the Labour and Co-operative Movements, and those who had not previously been politically active.

Inter-war 'new feminism', with its emphasis on the special needs of women did not therefore disappear in 1946 after the death of its chief architect, Eleanor Rathbone: its ideas were revived and reworked by the MWA in their arguments and campaigns for women's legal and economic equality in the home. Although not a large organisation, the MWA's campaigns for legislative change, and its analysis of women's economic position in the family represented a 'modern' face of feminism distinctive to the era.[9]

Beveridge and the Status of the Housewife

To understand this distinctive post-war face of feminism, it is important to set it in a wider social context. During the inter-war years concern about the declining birth rate raised fears that the population would fall below replacement level. Much professional and political attention was focused on married women's role as mothers. Encouraging women to stay at home and procreate was a major concern of the Royal Commission on Population,[10] and underlay proposals in the

Beveridge Report[11] to raise the status of the housewife.

Arguing that women's work in the home was 'vital ... in ensuring the adequate continuance of the British Race and of British Ideals in the world', Beveridge stressed the importance of changing the language used to describe women's domestic role.[12] Instead of 'adult dependants', married women should be seen as 'partners' in a marital team, engaged in work of an equal value to that of paid employment outside the home; housewives should therefore be defined as a separate category of worker, 'ungainfully employed' rather than 'unoccupied'. Given the different, albeit equal, nature of women's unpaid work in the home, the Beveridge Report recommended that social insurance provision take into account the particular risks married women faced on giving up paid work to become full-time housewives and mothers. Men's National Insurance contributions should therefore be paid on behalf of both partners, ensuring that husband *and* wife received state benefit in the event of male unemployment or sickness. However, deciding married women's entitlement to insurance against desertion or divorce proved more problematic and left many legal loopholes which provided fuel for feminist campaigns throughout the 1950s.

The Beveridge Report was seen as double edged by most contemporary feminists. They welcomed the attention and applause women's domestic work was receiving and the range of services the Beveridge Report and the Royal Commission on Population proposed to support it, but they were critical of the way in which welfare proposals made married women economically dependant on their husbands. The MWA argued that rhetoric such as Beveridge's did little to ease married women's unequal and oppressed economic position in the family, so long as they had no legal right to any part of the male income. Whilst some husbands might be generous with their money, women were still ultimately dependant on men's goodwill to receive a reasonable sum for housekeeping and, if lucky, a personal allowance. Since the 'family wage' was in reality an income owned and very often controlled by

61

one half of the marital team, the MWA demanded legislation
to secure the housewife's right to ownership of half the male
income. By the mid 1940s, it had amassed a sufficient list of
married women's economic grievances in their 'domestic
workshop' to style itself a Housewives Trade Union, and
attempt (unsuccessfully) affiliation to the Trades Union
Congress.

Feminism and Married Women's Economic Dependence

During the war, what became known as the Blackwell Case
was promoted by the MWA as striking evidence of married
women's economic dependence on men and of the urgent
need to remedy this inequality by legislation. Having saved
the dividend from shopping at her local Co-operative store
for many years, Mrs Blackwell was dispossessed of these
savings when her estranged husband claimed that since the
savings had been accumulated from money taken out of his
wages, he was legally entitled to them.[13] Media coverage of
the case, which the MWA took unsuccessfully to appeal, did
however boost membership of the Association in branches
throughout the country.

After the war the MWA took up issues stemming from the
distressed economic position of deserted and divorced
women. It campaigned for husbands' maintenance payments
to be deducted from wages at source in the event of
non-payment, and for women to have a legal right to the
marital home and its contents. There were however,
considerable differences within the organisation as to whether
divorce itself should be made easier. Some semblance of unity
was achieved by arguing instead for efforts to promote and
protect marriage, and by concentrating on the causes of
divorce (in their view women's economic dependence was a
source of marital conflict) and its economic effects on women
and children.

This approach resulted in some common ground and

contact with religious women's organisations such as the Mothers' Union, which feared that rising rates of divorce, illegitimacy and delinquency were threatening the survival of marriage and the family. Whilst some women in the MWA saw these links as a temporary alliance, others were keen to expand the scope of the group's work beyond its feminist aims of legal and financial equality. The Associations's Conservative chair, Lady Helen Nutting, felt the MWA would be 'far from fulfilling (its) mission' if it 'embraced nothing more fundamental than the dry bones of the law', and she urged members to concentrate on strengthening and protecting 'the very essence of the state', marriage and the family.[14]

Yet the MWA should not be seen simply as an organisation committed to the promotion and idealisation of marriage and family. Although it did not challenge the primacy of either institution in women's lives, it had begun to politicise the relationship between men and women within the family, by highlighting women's economic vulnerability in marriage together with the subsequent power imbalance this created between husbands and wives. It also claimed that it was taking feminism a stage further, and that its campaigns for married women's legal and financial rights were more relevant to working-class women than earlier feminist campaigns for property and political rights.[15] These attempts to politicise the personal or private sphere of home life, and to establish economic equality between husbands and wives clearly foreshadowed the concerns of post-1960s feminists, who identified the family as a major site of women's oppression.[16]

Where the MWA did not break new ground was in its methods for achieving change. Co-operation with women MPs (especially Labour's Edith Summerskill) and regular access to government ministries on deputations during the war seem to have convinced the leadership that if it continued to maintain these parliamentary contacts it could have some influence on government policy. However, this specialised and centralised work – drafting and amending Bills and cultivating contacts with establishment figures – was given priority above mobilising support for issues at a local level, and so left women in local branches without a clear role in the organisation.

Equal Pay as a Feminist Issue

Although after the war the issue of equal pay did not succeed in mobilising an active mass movement of women on the same scale as suffrage had done, the Equal Pay Campaign Committee (EPCC) did succeed in building a broad coalition of women's organisations in support of the principle. During the period 1945-55, when equal pay was introduced in the common classes of government service, feminists therefore struggled to continue this longstanding campaign and in the process established wider networks within which to work for it.[17]

During the Second World War more women than ever became involved in paid employment outside the home. Some entered areas of work which were traditional male preserves and although their number was limited, there was nonetheless a concern on the part of many women workers and some trade unions that women should be given the 'rate for the job' if they were doing the same or very similar work to men.[18]

By 1943 the Government was sufficiently concerned about the climate of support for equal pay in the country to hold a 'propaganda' meeting for women.[19] Praising women's war effort at this meeting, Churchill assured women that their contribution had 'definitely altered those social and sex balances which years of convention had established'. However, he was careful not to mention equal pay.[20] Frustrated by the Government's failure even to discuss this issue, a group of feminist organisations, women only unions and several women MPs decided to launch an Equal Pay Campaign Committee (EPCC) to put pressure on the Government to introduce equal pay in the common classes of is own service. However, the campaign was neatly deflected by the Government's decision in 1944 to set up a Royal Commission on Equal Pay, to which many of the Campaign Committee's constituent groups were invited to give evidence. The campaign was therefore postponed.

When the Royal Commission reported in 1946, hopes for political change were high among feminists. With Labour in power and a series of welfare reforms projected, the realisation of many feminist aims seemed imminent. Vera Brittain was later to speak of this period as a 'product of the women's revolution' and looked forward to the day when 'the old conflict between male and female will ultimately reach reconciliation in a new synthesis which is already in sight'.[21] During the war an unsuccessful attempt by feminist groups to pass an Equal Citizenship (Blanket) Bill to remove outstanding legal grievances in one fell swoop, had provided further evidence of feminist feeling that the struggle for legal equality was in its last stages.

Yet hopes that equal pay was to be implemented by the Labour government were soon dashed. The Government refused either to implement equal pay (even on the limited terms recommended by the Royal Commission) or to receive deputations from women's groups on the matter. The EPCC therefore determined to renew its campaign and broaden the base of its support to put pressure on the Government. The increasing demand for women's labour power after 1947 gave feminists a sense that women still had some bargaining power.

However, a fundamental weakness of the campaign was its failure to capture the support and co-operation of organised women in the Labour and Trade Union Movement; this alliance had been a crucial factor in the suffrage struggle. Although the Fabian Women's Group and individual members of the Labour Party as well as the other mainstream parties became involved in the EPCC, the main umbrella organisation of Labour women's groups, the Standing Joint Committee of Industrial Working Women's Organisations did not affiliate to the Committee. Nor did the cross party group of feminist MPs involved have strong links with organised women in their own parties.[22]

Although there was support for equal pay among women trade unionists, their leadership persuaded them not to go against Labour Party and TUC policy of wage restraint by campaigning for immediate implementation of equal pay. However, policy changed in 1951 when the TUC rejected government pay policy and passed a motion, from the Civil Service Clerical Association, to press for equal pay in government service. The strongest support for equal pay among women trade unionists came from white collar and professional women workers, many of whom belonged to women-only unions already affiliated to the EPCC.[23] The Committee's limited demand for immediate implementation of equal pay in the common classes of government service failed to address the more complex issue of equal pay in industry, or to make its arguments relevant to the mass of women who worked in jobs which could not be directly compared to men's.

Nevertheless, the EPCC did succeed in bringing together a wide range of women's organisations in support of equal pay. These included large groups like the National Council of Women and the Women's Institute, neither of which identified as feminist. It was from the support of these organisations that an affiliated membership of over four million was derived, although the impression this figure conveys of a large mass of women actively supporting equal pay is somewhat misleading.[24] The National Council of Women passed resolutions on equal pay and worked closely with the EPCC at a national level, but its members and constituent groups appear to have shown much less interest in the issue.[25]

In addition, although the Government's refusal to meet deputations on equal pay forced the Committee to consider new tactics and led to some attempts to mobilise support in the country, resulting for example, in a demonstration and high profile presentation of a petition, it was generally cautious in its approach. Fearful of losing the Government's goodwill and prejudicing its case for immediate implementation of a limited measure of equal pay, the EPCC regularly procrastinated over the timing of public meetings and demonstrations and resisted supporting wider demands for equal pay in industry.[26]

When in 1955 the Conservative Chancellor R.A. Butler agreed to phase in equal pay in the Civil Service over the course of seven years, the EPCC was divided in its response. While Thelma Cazalet Keir, the ex-Conservative MP who chaired the Committee, made plans to celebrate this achievement by inviting Butler as guest of honour to a 'Milestone Dinner', several feminist groups refused to attend arguing that: 'for such a modicum of justice, so hesitatingly granted after such a long time, it seems to us there is little to celebrate'.[27] However, without sufficient resources or even contacts with women in industry, they were unable to continue the struggle for equal pay, and so, unsatisfactorily resolved, the issue dropped off their agenda.

Feminism and Peace

In the immediate post-war years the future role of feminism became a topic of debate among politically active women. Some argued that the time for women-only organisations was over and that women should fight remaining issues within political parties. Younger women, keen to take up new opportunities for activity in local government were particularly attracted to this approach, anxious to be involved in implementing policy changes. Most felt this could best be achieved by working alongside men. Some young women even began to feel that the women's struggle was a thing of the past. Marghanita Laski summed up this feeling well when she claimed:

> I was born too late for the battle. Older and nobler women

pamphlets and books. Some served as shop-stewards or sat on JPCs. Many had had pre-war experience of campaigning, in hunger marches and tenants rent-strikes, or for Aid For Spain, or against Mosley's Blackshirts. Many had been Left Book Club members. Some were trade union activists, some Labour Party members, some Communists.

The role of the Communist Party in creating the mood which made Labour's victory possible, has frequently been ignored by historians. During the war Labour Party membership and organisation declined, while conversely the Communist Party grew rapidly, especially from 1942-44. This was in part because Communists were organised into workplace groups, some of those in war industry being of considerable size and influence. The party was not uniformly strong across the country, and groups were most influential where Communists had been active in the Amalgamated Engineering Union (AEU) from the early 1930s and where, consequently, there were good relations with union officials and Labour Party members. The strongest concentration of factory groups was in the engineering factory belt around west and north-west London, but they were significant also in south-east Essex, Manchester, Sheffield, the West Midlands, Oxford and Bristol; and in Scotland in Paisley, Greenock and Dundee.[17] They were, interestingly, areas where Labour made gains in 1945.

In these areas the Communist Party influenced shop-stewards and JPCs, and generated propaganda in favour of production, Anglo-Soviet solidarity, a Second Front in Europe and post-war social change. There were also Communist organisations in the Merchant Navy, the Fire Service and the railways, as well as groups, which included some well-known names, among actors, musicians and other artists. While political organisation was illegal in the Forces, in large camps Communists formed discussion groups, and kept in touch with local branches of their party. Overseas they made contact with Communist Parties where these existed, and with local Communists wherever they were.

11

struggled that I should be free, and did their work so well that I've never even bothered about being bound. Rights for women, so far as my generation is concerned, is a dead issue.[28]

Another pressure for change came from feminists on the left, involved in the Labour and Communist Parties or independent of party politics, who attempted to link feminism with the issue of peace, arguing that women's different perspectives on matters related to militarism and war meant they had a special contribution to make in campaigning for peace. From 1948 peace became an issue of considerable concern to many women fearful of German rearmament, Britain's H bomb tests and the intensification of the Cold War. However, although there was support within feminist groups for broadening their scope beyond equality measures, the issue of peace proved controversial.

The MWA strongly believed that 'the time has now come when we must realise that we have a contribution to human welfare which cannot be made by men'.[29] But it was not prepared to associate itself with the peace question which might be construed, in the intensity of Cold War politics, as support for Communism; whilst in 1951, after internal debate about the links between peace and equality and the inadvisability of supporting both, the Six Point Group determined to become a 'pure feminist' organisation concerned only with issues of 'unadulterated equality'.[30] Efforts to link peace with feminism had come to a head in the group in 1950 when the President, Edith Summerskill, (now Minister of National Insurance) resigned after her name appeared without permission on the top of a letter sent to MPs urging them to oppose the Government's support for the Korean War.[31] This shift in the Six Point Group towards a narrower interpretation of feminism led to the resignation of several independent socialists who had dominated the group's executive after the war. Some followed Sybil Morrison and Dora Russell into organisations associated with the peace movement, whilst others became more involved in the

Labour Party and local government.

Thus, in the 1950s established feminist groups such as the Women's Freedom League, Fawcett Society and the Six Point Group, having confined themselves to issues of direct equality between the sexes, found themselves without a major cause after the partial implementation of equal pay in 1955. Attempting to adapt to a situation in which it believed equality had almost been achieved, the Six Point Group urged its members to continue the struggle as 'watchdogs of equality'.[32]

On the other hand, the MWA, rejecting the view that 'equality of status lies along the road of sameness, of adopting men's standards and values as the human norm', continued to campaign for issues of equality within a sphere of difference.[33] Yet the failure of socialist feminist efforts in the late 1940s to build an active women's peace movement, meant that 'new' feminism remained in the safe and respectable territory of old pressure group tactics with a single issue or sectional approach. In the political climate of the Cold War, reluctant to associate feminism with anything that smacked of Communism, the MWA and other women's groups became increasingly isolated politically.[34] The MWA fought on for the many outstanding grievances suffered by women in the home, but failed to link these to other aspects of women's lives, even though increased numbers of women were now performing two roles in the home and in paid employment. It was not until the late 1950s that it began to accept these changing patterns.[35]

Nevertheless, the ideas and issues which the MWA promoted during the 1940s and 1950s show that this was not *simply* a period of decline and fragmentation in women's politics. By attempting to improve the status of women in the home, the MWA contributed to an understanding of the roots of women's oppression within the family. That they did not reject either the sexual division of labour in the home or suggest alternatives to the institution of marriage has tended to result in modern feminist histories emphasising the *differences* between feminism in the 1940s and 1950s and in the so-called Second Wave. There has been little acknowledgement of the ways in which the ideas and issues of post-war feminism foreshadowed some of the dominant concerns of the Women's Liberation Movement, notably its emphasis on the family as a primary site of women's oppression. By demanding a political solution to the economic inequality and dependence of full time housewives and mothers – a legal right to half the male income – the MWA was explicitly politicising the personal and private sphere of family and marital relations. In addition, by highlighting the vulnerability and power imbalance women suffered as a result of economic dependency in marriage, it was developing further an understanding of the roots of patriarchy within the private sphere.

Acknowledgements

Many thanks to Gillian Elinor for comments on earlier drafts of this chapter and to Sue Mew for her support and encouragement.

Notes

[1] Birmingham Feminist History 1979 Group, 'Feminism as femininity in the 1950s?' *Feminist Review*, Number 3; E. Wilson, *Only Halfway to Paradise*, Tavistock, London 1980.
[2] S. Rowbotham, *Women's Consciousness, Man's World*, Penguin, Harmondsworth, 1973, p3.
[3] See for example: R. Delmar, 'What is Feminism?' in J. Mitchell & A. Oakley (eds), *What is Feminism*, Blackwell, Oxford 1973; C. Ramazanoglu, *Contradictions of Oppression*, Routledge, London 1989.
[4] The argument that opposition to the sexual division of labour in the home need not be a prerequisite of feminist identity has already resulted in re-evaluations of the historical links between conservatism and feminism: A. Light, *Forever England: Femininity, Literature and Conservatism Between the Wars*, Routledge, London 1991; B. Campbell, *The Iron Ladies: Why Do Women Vote Tory?*, Virago, London 1987. Identification of 'pro-family' feminism in the 1980s lends further support to the view that

the ideas and issues of post-war feminists have been a persistent and legitimate strand in the history of feminism: J. Stacey, 'Are Feminists Afraid to Leave Home? The Challenge of Conservative Pro-Family Feminism' in J. Mitchell & A. Oakley (eds), *What is Feminism?*, Blackwell, Oxford 1986.

5 See for example: N. Black, *Social Feminism*, Cornell University Press, London 1989, and P. Thane, 'The Women of the British Labour Party and Feminism 1906-45' in H.L. Smith (ed), *British Feminism in the Twentieth Century*, Edward Elgar, London. Both argue that the term 'feminist' should be applied to particular women's organisations attached to the Labour Movement, since their ideas and issues overlap considerably with those of self-identified feminist organisations.

6 Both the National Council of Women and the Women's Institute supported equal pay during and after the war and were affiliated to the feminist led Equal Pay Campaign Committee. The Townswomen's Guild and the Women's Co-operative Guild also supported 'feminist' ideas and issues in the 1940s and 1950s.

7 The following women's groups identified themselves as feminist: Association for Social and Moral Hygiene; London and National Society (the Fawcett Society from 1953); Married Women's Association; Open Door Council; St. Joan's Social and Political Alliance; Six Point Group; Status of Women Committee; Suffragette Fellowship; Women For Westminster; Women's Freedom League.

8 The Married Women's Association was established as an independent organisation in 1938 and Women For Westminster in 1942, although the latter merged with the National Women's Citizens' Association in 1948.

9 In December 1945, according to the Association's journal *Wife & Citizen*, there were 2000 members, whilst in 1949 there were thirteen local branches according to Dora Russell, Chair of the organisation in 1950: D. Russell, (1985) *The Tamarisk Tree: Volume Three*, Virago, London 1985, p119.

10 *Report of the Royal Commission on Population*, HMSO, London 1949.

11 W. Beveridge, *Social Insurance and Allied Services*, HMSO, London 1942.

12 *Ibid.*, p53.

13 E. Summerskill, *A Woman's World: Her Memoirs*, Heinemann, London 1967, p144.

14 *Wife & Citizen*, July 1947.

15 Teresa Billington Grieg in MWA Newsletter, April 1954.

16 See for example: J. Mitchell, *Women's Estate*, Penguin, Harmondsworth 1971.

17 A. Potter, 'The Equal Pay Campaign Committee: A Case Study of a Pressure Group', *Political Studies*, Number 5, 1957. This article provides the only detailed account of the feminist struggle for equal pay in this period.

18 Support for equal pay from unions like the Amalgamated Engineers Union was however short lived. The demand for the 'rate for the job' was

71

seen as a temporary measure aimed at protecting the pay, conditions and status of 'men's' jobs during the war when women were entering 'male' areas of work. The title of the agreement the union reached with government and employers illustrates this point well: the Restoration of Pre-War Practices Act (1942).

[19] N. Soldon, *Women in British Trade Unions*, Gill & Macmillan, London 1978, pp149-50, notes that earlier in the year there were a few strikes related to demands for equal pay, including one in Glasgow which lasted a week; H.L. Smith 'The Womanpower Problem in Britain During the Second World War', *Historical Journal*, Number 27.4, 1984, p935 notes that Gallup Poll findings in 1943 discovered 68 per cent for equal pay and 26 per cent against.

[20] Smith, 1984, *op.cit.*, p925.

[21] V. Brittain, *Lady Into Woman*, Andrew Dakers, London 1953, pp8-11.

[22] Pugh, *op.cit.*, p170: Edith Summerskill had 'no significant base in the party', but was brought in to attract middle class votes in a suburban constituency.

[23] Soldon, *op.cit.*

[24] Smith, 1981, *op.cit.*, p667.

[25] Annual Reports of the National Council of Women 1947 and 1948.

[26] Equal Pay Campaign Committee minutes, Box 157, Fawcett Library.

[27] MWA Newsletter, 1956.

[28] Quoted in Pugh, *op.cit.*, p285.

[29] *Wife & Citizen*, December 1948.

[30] Letter to Sybil Morrison 24/7/50, Box 527, Fawcett Library.

[31] Russell, *op.cit.*, pp128-130.

[32] Six Point Group Newsletter, March 1954, Box 538, Fawcett Library.

[33] *Wife & Citizen*, December 1948.

[34] Birmingham Feminist History Group, *op.cit.*

[35] A. Myrdal & V. Klein, *Women's Two Roles*, Routledge & Kegan Paul, London, 1956. This feminist text, one of the few published in the post-war years, marked an important development in post-war feminist thought. Although it did not assert married women's 'right' to paid work, preferring to see it as 'duty' to the community (J. Lewis, 'Myrdal, Klein, Women's Two Roles and Post War Feminism 1945-60' in H.L. Smith (ed), *British Feminism in the Twentieth Century*, Elgar, Aldershot 1989) it did acknowledge and positively endorse the increasing numbers of married women and mothers engaged in paid employment outside the home.

A 'Third Way'?:
The Labour Left, Democratic Socialism and the Cold War

Jonathan Wood

> There is only one hope for mankind – and that is democratic Socialism.
>
> Aneurin Bevan; Speech of Resignation from
> the Cabinet, 23 April 1951

The ideology of the Labour Left has been distinguished by a commitment to the socialist transformation of society, as opposed to social amelioration within the existing capitalist framework, and by the conviction that socialism could be achieved by parliamentary means.[1] In the 1930s the rise of Fascism throughout Europe led many of Labour's left-wingers to fear that parliamentary Socialism might be defeated by illegal and violent opposition from the ruling-class,[2] but Labour's overwhelming electoral victory of 1945, and the successful implementation of major reforms, gave the Labour Left renewed faith in the parliamentary road.[3]

Economic Strategy

The economic strategy of the post-war Labour Left was based on planning, economic controls and public ownership of all the major industries. Aneurin Bevan, writing in wartime, considered it vital to ensure 'that the dominant role in society is played by public ownership ...'[4] Full employment and an efficient economy were unattainable without public ownership of the main economic sectors. Political democracy itself could survive only if the economy were under democratic control. Sybil Wingate, a left-wing activist, told the 1945 Labour Party Conference, '... You cannot give full employment if you leave heavy industry in private hands, or keep a Labour government in office if you leave big business alone'.[5] Bevan warned that, 'a political democracy, based on private ownership of industry, finance and commerce, is an essentially unstable society'.[6]

The industries nationalised by the Labour government were organized as public corporations, with managing boards which were appointed by the appropriate Ministers. The workers and trade unions were not directly represented on the managing boards, a policy accepted by the TUC General Council.[7] However, several unions, most notably the National Union of Railwaymen (NUR) and the Union of Post Office Workers (UPW), which had been strongly influenced by the ideas of the Guild Socialists, advocated workers' participation in the management of the nationalised industries.[8] Left-wingers generally wanted the Labour government to make greater use of planning and physical controls of economic activity, and favoured the expansion of public ownership and the introduction of industrial democracy.

The influential pamphlet *Keep Left*, written by three Labour MPs, Richard Crossman, Michael Foot and Ian Mikardo, and published in May 1947, expressed the views of the fifteen Labour MPs belonging to the 'Keep Left' group.[9] It emphasised the need for proper overall economic planning, recommended an economic strategy based on government intervention and the extensive use of economic controls, and called for the nationalisation of every industry which had a hold over the national economy or could not be made efficient under private ownership.[10] The 'Keep Left' group believed in industrial democracy and proposed an expanded version of the wartime Joint Production Committees. These were advisory bodies which had been established in industry during the Second World War and enabled workers' representatives to participate in planning production: these should be made compulsory in all but the smallest establishments, and given greatly increased powers.[11]

After 1948, the Labour government, on the other hand, became increasingly open in its acceptance of a mixed economy in which the private sector predominated. Herbert Morrison proposed limiting further nationalisation to allow the Government to concentrate on improving and consolidating the existing public sector, and the Labour Party leadership adopted this philosophy.[12] The Government abandoned physical controls as a method of economic planning and moved towards a Keynesian economic policy.[13]

By this time, most of Labour's left-wingers were willing to agree to a halt in further major measures of nationalisation (with the exception of iron and steel) and accept the idea of a mixed economy. Richard Crossman stated that the Labour Party would not oppose an end to further large-scale nationalisation once the steel industry had been taken into public ownership.[14] In 1950, the sequel to *Keep Left*, *Keeping Left*, was much more cautious in its attitude to further nationalisation than its predecessor and argued that there was universal agreement that Britain would have a 'mixed' economy for a long time to come.[15]

However, the Labour Left had not reconciled itself to capitalist ownership of the bulk of the economy or to the dominance of market forces continuing indefinitely. G.D.H. Cole, socialist intellectual and Chairman of the Fabian Society, deprecated acceptance of a 'mixed economy' as 'a permanent resting-place' and asserted that a mixed economy based on the continued existence of capitalism in much of industry was unworkable in the long run.[16] Bevan was convinced that unless elected representatives had effective control over economic affairs, parliamentary democracy would be undermined by its inability to remedy economic problems.[17] *Keeping Left* considered financial and physical controls essential for a successful economic strategy. Economic planning, it argued, had to recognise that the free market system was outdated.

The public corporations controlling the nationalised industries were frequently criticised. *Keeping Left* argued that they were the main reason for the public sector's failure to meet Socialists' expectations. Nationalisation had not produced a greater degree of workers' participation in management; joint consultative committees should be legally compulsory.[18] This approach, based on joint consultation, was very different from the more radical vision of the Guild Socialists or the policies of the UPW, the NUR and other left-wing unions which demanded workers' participation in the management of the nationalised industries. The UPW proposed that a Joint Administrative Council, half of whose members would be representatives from the staff associations, be created to manage the Post Office.[19] The differences between trade union advocates of workers' participation and the parliamentary Labour Left were outlined in a Fabian Tract *Consultation or Joint Management*, which contained contributions from J.M. Chalmers, editor of the UPW's journal the *Post*, Ian Mikardo MP and G.D.H. Cole. Chalmers defended his union's advocacy of joint management and contended that joint-consultation did not give workers a democratic share in decision-making. Mikardo and Cole disagreed with this. In Mikardo's opinion, joint consultation properly operated was the only possible form of joint management. Cole pointed to the serious problems, including conflict of interests, raised by the UPW's concept of a Joint Administrative Council.[20]

These debates revealed the disagreements over such issues as the feasibility of trade unions exercising managerial responsibility while defending their members' interests and the risk of elected workers' representatives on managing boards facing a conflict between their responsibility to the workers and their duty to the community.[21] The Labour Left was deeply divided over the appropriate structures for industrial democracy.

A Socialist Foreign Policy

The basic assumptions of the Labour Left's view of foreign policy were that war was the product of capitalism and that building Socialism in Britain and pursuing a socialist foreign policy were closely connected and interdependent.[22] A Labour government should make a complete break with traditional British foreign policy. Leonard Woolf argued in 1944 that the Tories' economic and international policy was responsible for the war and had to be reversed completely.[23]

In 1945 the Labour Party as a whole believed that lasting peace and stability depended on close co-operation between the USA, USSR, and Britain.[24] Additionally, the Left thought that only a reconstruction of European society based on socialist principles could succeed, and hoped for a close alliance between Labour and the political forces which had participated in the European resistance movements.[25] In fact, the Cold War ended any possibility of Britain, the USA, and the USSR working together. Ernest Bevin, Labour's Foreign Secretary, pursued a strongly anti-Communist and anti-Soviet policy and Britain allied itself with the USA against the Soviet Union. This produced ideological division within the Labour left. A pro-Soviet grouping vigorously defended the Soviet Union's policies, opposed Bevin's foreign policy and urged the Government to adopt a policy of friendship and co-operation with the Soviet Union. Konni Zilliacus, MP for Gateshead, was the most eloquent of these Sovietophile Labour MPs, arguing that the Labour government had to choose between international unity with the USSR in working for peace, or national unity with the Tories in drifting into the Third World War. He proposed that the

Labour government seek agreement with the Soviet Union on encouraging co-operation between all Socialist parties and promoting unity of action between Socialists and Communists.[26] This pro-Soviet element, a minority within the Labour Left, became politically isolated as the Cold War polarized opinion within the Labour Movement.

Much more influential were those left-wingers who espoused a 'Third Force' policy. They maintained that democratic socialist Britain should follow a 'middle way' between capitalist America and communist Russia and lead a Third Force, based on a democratic socialist western Europe, independent of, and able to mediate between, the two superpowers.[27] A lucid and cogent statement of Third Force ideas was provided by *Keep Left*, denouncing the idea of 'collective security against communism' as threatening to divide Europe into rival spheres of influence and lead ultimately to a Third World War. Britain had to remain independent of the American and Soviet camps in order to facilitate reconciliation between the USA and the USSR and save smaller nations from the ideological conflict between the superpowers. An independent Britain could avert war. 'Keep Left' favoured a close alliance between Britain and France, which, with the Commonwealth, could prevent the division of Europe and the world into hostile blocs[28].

However, international political developments quickly made such recommendations outdated. The USA's Marshall Plan, which supplied American aid to support European recovery, and the Soviet Union's rejection of and campaign against Marshall Aid resulted in an intensification of the Cold War. Britain joined in the formation of the Atlantic Pact. Marshall Aid and Soviet oppression in eastern Europe brought radical changes in Labour Left attitudes to the two superpowers. Most of the left-wingers who had supported 'Third Force' ideas identified themselves, however reluctantly, with the Anglo-American alliance and its policy of opposing Soviet Communism.[29] Those leftists who still defended the Soviet Union became vulnerable to disciplinary action. Zilliacus and three other pro-Soviet Labour MPs were expelled from the Party,[30] and pro-Soviet political sentiment ceased to be a significant force within the Labour Party.[31]

Nonetheless, many left-wingers were unwilling to acquiesce in extremely high military expenditure or condone the fanatical anti-Communism prevalent in the USA. An alternative foreign policy was put forward in *Keeping Left*, which maintained that the West's internal political and economic tensions were a much greater threat than the possibility of Soviet military aggression. It claimed that the Soviet leaders hoped internal forces would cause the social and economic disintegration of the western nations, allowing the Soviet Union to extend its control without military conflict. Heavy arms expenditure which exacerbated socio-economic problems would increase the West's insecurity. The first line of defence was social and economic while military strength was only the second line.

Heavy emphasis was placed on the role of the colonial and recently decolonised countries in global politics. '*Keeping Left*' asserted; 'The major fact of the world today is that the coloured peoples ... are in social revolution against the ideas symbolized by White Ascendancy and European Imperialism'. It advocated British recognition of, and assistance for, people who had liberated themselves by revolution, so as to enable social revolutionary movements to become independent of the Kremlin. Socialists had to identify with the social revolution of the colonial masses.[32]

Bevanism: Democratic Socialism and the Cold War

Britain responded to the Korean War of 1950 and growing Cold War tensions with a massively increased re-armament programme, to help finance which charges on National Health Service teeth and eye treatment were introduced in the Budget of April 1951. Three Ministers, Aneurin Bevan, Harold Wilson and John Freeman, resigned in protest. These three joined forces with the left-wing Labour MPs who had produced *Keeping Left*, so creating the Bevanite group, which during 1951 issued two widely-read and controversial pamphlets '*One Way Only*' and '*Going Our Way*'.[33] Bevanism rallied a wide range of left-wing opinion behind its leadership and united a Labour Left which had been fragmented since 1945.[34]

The left-wing belief that domestic policy and foreign policy were interdependent was a central tenet of Bevanism. *One Way Only* declared that it was no longer possible to believe that 'home affairs' and 'foreign affairs' had no connection with one another, and concluded that putting right Britain's political relations abroad was the main solution to her economic problems.[35]

Bevanism shared many of the ideas and assumptions of the 'Keep Left' Group and of *Keeping Left*, especially in foreign policy. The resignation speeches of Bevan and Wilson, describing Britain as showing the world an alternative to US capitalism and Soviet communism, revealed the influence of 'Third Force' ideas.[36] The Bevanites conceded that Soviet Communism presented a threat to the West and that some degree of re-armament was necessary, but argued that the seriousness of the Soviet military threat was greatly exaggerated and the Soviet bloc was much weaker, both militarily and economically, than the West.[37] The Soviet threat was social, economic and ideological rather than military. Hence, excessive re-armament which aggravated the West's social and economic difficulties offered much greater opportunities to Soviet Communism than military aggression. Consequently, the huge increases in military expenditure to combat Soviet Communism were counter-productive.[38]

The importance of the underdeveloped countries in world politics figured as prominently in Bevanite literature as it had done in *Keeping Left*. 'The social revolution in Asia, Africa and the Middle East is the dominant fact of the twentieth century'.[39] Britain had to align itself with the forces of social revolution in the colonial world, and a major programme of aid which alleviated poverty would be a far better guarantee of global peace than arms spending. If the West opposed or failed to support the social revolution in the underdeveloped countries, the colonial masses might be driven to embrace Communism and join the Soviet camp.[40]

The Bevanites believed public ownership was essential for establishing Socialism in Britain. The problems of planning Britain's economy could not be solved, asserted Bevan, until the power relations between public and private property had been drastically altered. He recognised the fact that most people in the West preferred a mixed economy, but argued that public property had to be the dominant form of property ownership.[41] The shortcomings of the existing nationalised industries were recognised. Crossman noted that the state-owned industries had retained the old pre-nationalisation managements almost unaltered.[42] In Bevan's view, public ownership was only the first step towards Socialism, and, in western societies, industrial democracy was the counterpart of political freedom.[43] However, no detailed proposals for the democratisation of the public sector were produced.[44]

Bevan acknowledged his intellectual debt to Marxism but thought that classical Marxism had consistently under-estimated the role of political democracy. He saw the function of parliamentary democracy as exposing 'wealth-privilege to the attack of the people'.[45]

The influence of the Cold War on Bevanite ideology was revealed by the way in which the differences between democratic Socialism and Soviet Communism were empha-sised. The central feature of world politics, according to John Freeman, was the battle of ideas between Soviet Communism and western democratic Socialism, the latter's fullest expression being the British Labour Party.[46] Richard Crossman contrasted the historical determinism of the Communists, who believed historical forces guaranteed their victory, with the conviction of democratic socialists that only human will and social conscience could avert slavery, war and exploitation.[47]

The influential theory of the managerial society, which claimed that control of industry was passing from traditional capitalist entrepreneurs to professional managers, had a significant impact on the Bevanites, who feared that the rise of the managerial society threatened basic freedoms. Crossman considered it the greatest current enemy of freedom, while Bevan warned that the managerial society would leave the citizen 'the passive creature of a class of supposed supermen' presenting themselves as public servants.[48] Soviet Communism and the managerial society were opposed because freedom and its expansion was a vital element in Bevanism's democratic socialist philosophy: 'Enlargement of freedom ... is socialism's highest aim', affirmed Crossman. Socialism's main task was to prevent the concentration of power in the hands of either industrial management or the state bureaucracy, distribute responsibility and thus enlarge freedom of choice.[49]

Bevan and his supporters emphasised their commitment to maintaining Party unity.[50] *One Way Only* stated that it was not an alternative programme for the Labour Movement and that only the Labour Party's Annual Conference could make policy.[51] In 1945, the Labour Party leadership had been identified with the doctrine that public ownership was superior to private enterprise but had abandoned this viewpoint by 1951.[52] The Bevanites wanted to maintain this commitment to public ownership. Rather than producing new policies, they claimed to be defending well-established socialist beliefs and values which the Party leadership was discarding.

Socialism and Democracy

The Labour Left believed parliamentary democracy could be used to create a democratic socialist Britain in which democracy would no longer be confined to the political sphere but would be extended into industry and every form of social activity. G.D.H. Cole expressed the left's aspirations when he wrote;

> For democracy is an integral part of Socialism – and not merely that almost passive democracy which finds expression in the right to vote, but very much more than that. A Socialist democracy will be a society in which every individual counts ... Such a society cannot exist unless it is permeated in all its parts by the democratic spirit.[53]

The ultimate aim was economic and social democracy based on popular participation. Richard Crossman regarded democracy which grew from the bottom upwards as a fundamental principle of British Socialism; '... the traditions of British social democracy are based on the voluntary organisation ... the essence of British democracy is this voluntary, spontaneous organisation from below'.[54] Democracy rather than public ownership was the criterion of Socialism. 'Our social democracy is now based not merely on public ownership ... but also on the destruction of arbitrary power, whether exercised by the manager, the bureaucrat or the State'.[55]

The consolidation of the mixed economy and the advent of the Cold War frustrated left-wing hopes for democratic socialism. Internal weaknesses also contributed to the left's failure. After Bevan's resignation, the Labour left lacked a credible leader and mass support among the Party's rank-and-file.[56] Left-wing proposals for a socialist economic strategy based on public ownership were discredited by the absence of public support for further large-scale nationalisation.[57] The Labour left's preoccupation with foreign policy in the late 1940s limited its appeal to the majority of Labour Party members, who were mainly concerned with domestic issues,[58] while left-wing opposition to the Government's foreign policy was deeply divided ideologically. The Cold

War exacerbated these divisions, producing conflict within the Left.[59] Nevertheless, despite political defeats, Labour leftists continued to argue that Socialism and democracy were indissolubly linked.

Notes

[1] Patrick Seyd, *The Rise and Fall of the Labour Left*, Macmillan Education, London 1987, pp1-2; Leo Panitch, *Social Democracy and Industrial Militancy; The Labour Party, the Trade Unions and Incomes Policy*, Cambridge University Press, 1976, p255.

[2] Geoffrey Foote, *The Labour Party's Political Thought, A History*, Croom Helm, Beckenham 1985, pp154, 158-9; Frank Bealey (ed), *The Social and Political Thought of the British Labour Party*, Weidenfeld and Nicholson, London 1970, pp137-8.

[3] See e.g. Richard Crossman in 'Victory Conference', *New Statesman* (NS), 15 June 1946, and 'Socialist Stocktaking 111 – Planning and Controls' *NS*, 6 November 1948.

[4] 'Celticus' (Aneurin Bevan), *Why not Trust the Tories*, Gollancz, London 1944, p87.

[5] Report of Forty-Fourth Annual Conference of the Labour Party, 21st-25th May 1945, p134.

[6] Bevan, *op.cit.*, p87.

[7] Eirene White, *Workers' Control*, Fabian Publications and Gollancz, London 1951, p5; Austen Albu, 'The Organisation of Industry' in R.H.S Crossman (ed), *New Fabian Essays*, Turnstile Press, London 1952, Dent, London 1970, p125; 'Workers' Control of Industry and the British Labour Party', *American Political Science Review*, October 1947, pp893-900.

[8] P.S. Bagwell, *The Railwaymen: Vol 2: The Beeching Era and After*, Allen and Unwin, London 1982, p327; J.M. Chalmers, Ian Mikardo, and G.D.H. Cole, *Consultation or Joint Management?* Fabian Society, London 1949, pp12, 14, 25; White, *op.cit.*, pp13-14.

[9] R. Crossman, M. Foot, I. Mikardo, *Keep Left*, New Statesman, London 1947.

[10] *Ibid*, pp11, 26, 46.

[11] *Ibid*, pp24-25; Kurt L. Shell, 'Industrial Democracy and the British Labour Movement', *Political Science Quarterly*, Vol. 72, No. 4, December 1957, pp527-8.

[12] Herbert Morrison, 'The Recent General Election and the Next', NEC Minutes, 22 March 1950; L.D. Epstein, 'Socialism and the British Labour Party', *Political Science Quarterly*, Vol. 66, No. 4, December 1951, pp559-62.

[13] P. Addison, *The Road to 1945; British Politics and the Second World*

War, Quartet Books, London 1977, p274; K.O. Morgan, *Labour in Power*, OUP, Oxford 1985, p364.

[14] R.H.S. Crossman, 'Memorandum on Problems Facing the Party', NEC Minutes, 26 April 1950.

[15] *Keeping Left, Labour's First Five Years and the Problems Ahead*, by a Group of MPs, New Statesman Publications, London 1950, pp29, 32.

[16] G.D.H. Cole, 'The Dream and the Business', *Political Quarterly*, Vol. 20, Nos 1-4, 1949, pp205-6; G.D.H. Cole, *Labour's Second Term; a Comment on the Draft 'Labour Believes in Britain'*, Fabian Tract No. 273, Fabian Publications, London 1949, p17.

[17] Aneurin Bevan, *Democratic Values*, Fabian Tract no. 282, Fabian Publications, London 1951, pp7-8.

[18] *Keeping Left, op.cit.*, pp14-15, 29-31, 36-7.

[19] White, *op.cit.*, p7.

[20] Chalmers, Mikardo and Cole, *op.cit.*, pp7-28.

[21] G.D.H. Cole, *The National Coal Board; Its Tasks, Its Organisation and Its Prospects*, Fabian Research Series No. 129, Fabian Publications and Gollancz, London 1948, pp6-13; Chalmers, Mikardo and Cole, *op.cit.*, pp9-14, 17-18, 20, 23, 26; White, *op.cit.*, pp11, 25-6, 29.

[22] See e.g. Harold Laski, Foreword to Leonard Woolf, *Foreign Policy; the Labour Party's Dilemma'* Fabian Publications, London 1947, pp3-4.

[23] Leonard Woolf, *The International Post-War Settlement*, Fabian Research Series No. 85, Fabian Publications, London 1944, p3.

[24] See e.g. Woolf, *International Post-War Settlement, cit.* pp12-13; Konni Zilliacus, *Why I was Expelled: Bevinism vs Election Pledges, Socialism and World Peace*, Narod Press, London 1949, p10; speeches by Ian Mikardo and Michael Stewart, Labour Party Annual Conference Report, 1945, pp93, 96-7, 100.

[25] Woolf, *International Post-War, cit.*, pp20-21; Zilliacus, *op.cit.*, pp10-34; John Freeman, speech, Labour Party Annual Conference Report 1945, p100.

[26] Konni Zilliacus, *Britain, the USSR and World Peace*, British–Soviet Society, London 1946, pp25-6, 34.

[27] Jonathan Schneer, 'Hopes Deferred or Shattered: the British Labour Left and the Third Force Movement, 1946-49, *Journal of Modern History*, Vol 26, No 2, June 1984, p198.

[28] *Keep Left, cit*, pp34-5, 38, 46-7.

[29] *Keeping Left, cit*, p25; Douglas Hill, *Tribune: the First Forty Years of a Socialist Newspaper*, Quartet Books, London 1977, p69; 'A London Diary' by Critic, *NS*, 10 July 1948.

[30] NEC Meeting, Sub-Committee of Officers and Chairmen of Sub-Committees; Discussion of Activities of John Platts-Mills and the Nenni Telegram, NEC Minutes, 28 April 1948; Supplementary Report of NEC to Party Conference, 1949, Expulsions of Konni Zilliacus and L.J. Solley, NEC Minutes, June 1949; Expulsion of Lester Hutchinson, NEC Minutes, July 1949; Zilliacus, *Why I was Expelled, cit*, pp3-5, 21-53.

[31] R. Crossman, 'At Margate', *NS*, 7 October 1950; 'Loyalty Beat "Red Sheep" ', *London News*, January 1950, London Labour Party Papers, 1950.

[32] *Keeping Left*, pp20-22, 23, 25, 44.

[33] Mark Jenkins, *Bevanism: Labour's High Tide. The Cold War and the Democratic Mass Movement*, Spokesman University paperback, Nottingham 1981, pp148-9, 80, 153.

[34] J. Schneer, *Labour's Conscience: the Labour Left 1945–51*, Unwin Hyman, London 1988, pp203-7.

[35] *One Way Only: A Socialist Analysis of the Present World Crisis*, with foreword by Aneurin Bevan, Harold Wilson and John Freeman, Tribune Publications, London 1951, p13.

[36] Parliamentary Debates, 5th Series, Vol. 487, Col. 38, Aneurin Bevan's resignation speech (23 April 1951); Col. 231, Harold Wilson's resignation speech (24 April 1951).

[37] *One Way Only*, *cit.*, p9; *Going Our Way*, contributions from Aneurin Bevan, Harold Wilson and John Freeman, Tribune Publications, London 1951, pp12, 14-5; Aneurin Bevan, *In Place of Fear*, Quartet Books, London 1952, pp160-1.

[38] Parliamentary Debates, *cit.*, Col. 37, Bevan's resignation speech; *One Way Only*, *cit.*, p10; *Going Our Way*, *cit.*,, p13.

[39] *One Way Only*, *cit.*, p4.

[40] Aneurin Bevan speech, Report of Annual Conference of Labour Party 1951, p121; R. Crossman, 'Towards a Philosophy of Socialism,' in *New Fabian Essays*, *cit.*, pp17, 22-25.

[41] Bevan, *In Place of Fear*, *cit.*, pp144-5.

[42] Crossman, 'Towards a Philosophy' *cit.*, p27.

[43] Bevan, *In Place of Fear*, *cit.*, p130.

[44] David Howell, *The Rise and Fall of Bevanism*, Labour Party Discussion Series No. 5, ILP, Square One Publications, Leeds n.d.

[45] Bevan, *In Place of Fear*, *cit.*, p25.

[46] *Going Our Way*, *cit.*, p11.

[47] Crossman, *Towards a Philosophy*, *cit.*, p15.

[48] *Ibid*, p12; Bevan, *In Place of Fear*, *cit.*, pp127-8.

[49] Crossman, *Towards a Philosophy*, *cit.*, pp27, 29.

[50] Parliamentary Debates, *cit*, Col 231, Wilson's resignation speech; Bevan, speech, Labour Party Annual Conference Report 1951.

[51] *One Way Only*, *cit.*, p16.

[52] Epstein, *op.cit.*, pp556-62.

[53] Cole, *Labour's Second Term*, *cit.*, p14.

[54] R. Crossman, *Socialist Values in a Changing World*, Fabian Tract No. 286, Fabian Publications and Gollancz, London 1951, p6.

[55] *Keeping Left*, *cit.*, p28.

[56] See Jonathan Wood, doctoral thesis, *The Labour Left and the Constituency Labour Parties 1931-1951*, University of Warwick 1983, pp270-1, 275-6, 282-6; Crossman, 'Victory Conference' *cit.*; Martin Harrison, *Trade Unions and the Labour Party since 1945*, Allen and

persistent demands for equality; the Clerical and Administrative Workers' Union, which had grown so fast during the war, was to the forefront of the campaign. The Government refused both legislation and action in the Civil Service, whilst accepting the principle. The women's leadership again chose not to embarrass the Government; the Standing Joint Committee of Women Workers (SJC) representatives gave evidence to the Royal Commission on Equal Pay (1944-1946) but succumbed to pressure in 1948, recognising the Government's economic difficulties.[15] On this issue there was a rebellion at Women's Conference but the majority decided on Party first.

At the TUC, women's persistence was better rewarded. The TUC had regularly supported equal pay resolutions, although some women trade unionists were sceptical about the extent of TUC commitment.[16] In 1947 the 'weak and unconvincing attitude' of the General Council was protested. In 1950, when there had still been no action, the General Council plea for restraint 'in the national interest' was overturned by Congress. The following year the General Council itself lost patience with the Government's latest argument, that the claim for equal pay ought to be offset against gains in social services, reiterating that equal pay was a wage claim demanding immediate action.[17]

On the only occasion when the equal pay demand was pushed to a card vote at Labour Party Conference and won (2,310,000 for; 598,000 against) the leadership had already entered the caveat, 'it will ... continue to be the function of Government to plan legislation in the circumstances as they find them'.[18] Yet the simultaneous drive to win women for industry rendered the Government attitude more complex than simple perpetuation of the stereotype of the woman worker as both reluctant and temporary. In addition, it should be noted that discrimination was the result of the demarcation of jobs by gender; SJC Commissioners had found that where piece rates were paid there was little difference in men's and women's earnings. Also, as Amabel

Towards Isolation: The Communist Party and the Labour Government

John Callaghan

> The enemies of Communism accuse the Communist Party of aiming to introduce Soviet Power in Britain and abolish Parliament. This is a slanderous misrepresentation of our policy.
>
> *The British Road to Socialism*; Programme of the Communist Party of Great Britain, 1951

The Communist Party of Great Britain (CPGB) emerged from the war a bigger organisation than at any time before 1939. Of its 45,435 members, moreover, at least 85 per cent had been recruited since the adoption of the Popular (or People's) Front policy endorsed by the Seventh Congress of the Communist International (Comintern) in 1935. For almost ten years, in accordance with this policy, the Party membership had become accustomed to advocacy of the broadest possible alliance of anti-Fascists and during this period the organisation strove to situate itself within the national-popular tradition of radicalism in Britain. It was an orientation which was kept alive even during the period of the Party's opposition to the war from October 1939 to June 1941 in the form of the People's Convention. In the process some of the accoutrements of Bolshevism were dropped – the

Comintern itself was dissolved in 1943. The Party had never been better placed, or so it seemed, to take its place as a legitimate component of the Labour Movement. The Soviet Union had never been more favourably perceived in Britain – the first socialist state had played the major part in the destruction of Nazi Germany and this could not but reflect favourably upon a social and economic system allegedly superior to capitalism.[1] In the context, then, of the reflected glory of the Red Army and the mood of radicalism sweeping across Europe and Asia, the British Communists had reason to be confident.

Indeed even after a disappointing showing in the 1945 General Election – just two Communist MPs elected – the revived Party journal, *Modern Quarterly*, remained convinced, in the words of its first editorial, that 'we are living in a revolution'.[2]

The range of theoretical issues and distinguished contributors to be found in its pages testified to the richer political culture created in the Party since the Popular Front turn. The journal's enthusiasm for history, aesthetics, philosophy, art and science in part reflected its formal rejection of the idea that culture was simply an epiphenomenon of economic events.[3] But it was also evidence of confidence in the intellectual dominance of socialist thought and Marxism in particular. The 'People's War' had given birth to such a convincing swing to the left, moreover, that socialist hegemony looked set to last for at least twenty-five years to come. Little wonder, then, that a sense of 'revolution' was in the air.

Welcome to Labour's Victory

The Communists had demanded a 'popular victory' with an 'overwhelming majority of Labour and progressive MPs behind it' – preferably in the form of a 'Labour and progressive electoral alliance' or People's Front. The momentary enthusiasm which some Party leaders displayed in the spring of 1945 for a continuation of the coalition – no doubt in deference to Soviet propaganda concerning the 'lasting amity' of the 'Big Three' – was forgotten and R. Palme Dutt, the most loyal voice of Moscow within the CPGB leadership, welcomed the General Election result as 'a grand clearing-out operation'. It was nothing less than 'a glorious political leap forward', in Dutt's authoritative view – 'the counterpart to the sweep to the Left throughout Europe'.[4]

Ordinary Party members had even more reason than Dutt to regard Labour's victory as their own having provided a substantial proportion of the 'barrack-room lawyers' whose socialist agitation was widely believed to have shifted wartime opinion to the left. When the first post-war Congress took place in 1945 delegates angrily reminded the leadership of its earlier support for a renewed National government. But they were also worried by the Party's loss of distinctiveness in relation to Labour . After all, their own election policy was strikingly similar to Labour's in many respects. It stressed the need for nationalisation of coal, steel, power, inland transport and land; it wanted a national medical service and comprehensive social security, full employment, a massive housing programme and guaranteed prices for agricultural produce. Party leaders wrote in support of Beveridge's proposals.[5] In a perfunctory way – again like Labour – the Party referred to the need for planning; it talked of a 'Five Year Plan' that would re-equip industry and direct capital investment and on this basis envisaged 'compelling big business and monopoly to work on lines laid down by the Government in the interests of the nation'.[6] The non-Leninist assumptions and language employed here were also in evidence in Communist commentary on the King's Speech, which was judged to have 'won a universal welcome from all sections of the working-class movement and from the broadest sections of democratic opinion'. Dutt was even content to call for no more than 'the practical implementation' of the promise of self-government for India, Ceylon and Burma, omitting to mention his earlier doubts on the feasibility of such constitutional change and all reference to other territories demanding independence.[7] The momentum for Communist participation in parliamentary systems – begun in 1935 and carried forward during the later stages of the war by Stalin's foreign policy – continued well into the peace as Dutt's conciliatory remarks suggest; by 1947 Harry Pollitt, General Secretary of the CPGB, was able to explain that a 'British road to socialism' could be both peaceful and gradual, requiring neither soviets nor a dictatorship of the proletariat.[8]

Divergence on Foreign Policy

But on many matters of foreign policy wide divergences persistently separated Communist and official Labour opinion. Even at the height of Soviet-orchestrated support for the 'spirit of Teheran' – with its perspective of permanent collaboration between the Big Three – there were grounds for Communist concern in the Coalition's foreign policy. British policy in India, for example, was consistently likened to one of 'the worst military fiascos of the war' because the Government's refusal to grant independence was held responsible for the campaign of civil disobedience which Gandhi launched in August 1942.[9]

The Communists also suspected all sorts of Conservative intrigues in the deal which the Americans concluded with Admiral Darlan in French North Africa in the autumn of that year; they naturally noted with some anxiety media talk concerning the spectre of 'the supposed menace of a Soviet domination of Europe' with its implied threat of a resumption of anti-Bolshevik belligerence. Plenty of blemishes of this type defaced the picture of harmony concocted at Teheran and Yalta.[10]

The decision to send troops to Greece in December 1944 was certainly regarded as the most grotesque example of this seamier side of British policy – even though Stalin viewed it

91

with equanimity, having already agreed to give Britain free reign in that country. Harry Pollitt immediately condemned the anti-Communist intervention as a declaration of 'full-scale war against the Greek people' and saw at once that the Labour Ministers in the War Cabinet were the joint architects of Churchill's policy. It was already apparent that if Communist governments came to be formed in Italy and France after the war external intervention to topple them could be expected, if not to anticipate their formation as in Greece.[11] In July 1945 Pollitt was also obliged to note media prophecies that 'the next war will be with Russia' as conflict over the post-war settlement in Poland and Austria came to the surface again. As soon as Attlee's Government was formed, the Left could see that Labour had no intention of recalling General Scobie's army from Greece and at the London Conference of September 1945, where there were well-publicised acrimonious exchanges between Bevin and Molotov, the Communists perceived that a 'Western Bloc' excluding the Soviet Union was actually emerging.[12] At the Eighteenth Congress of the CPGB in November, it was stressed that Bevin's reactionary foreign policy threatened to wreck 'the over-all economic plan' required in Britain. But the emphasis was on 'threatened'; as long as the Soviet leaders continued to believe that a satisfactory *modus vivendi* was possible with the USA, the conduct of British foreign policy was not allowed to negate the CP's positive assessment of Labour's domestic programme.

Support on the Domestic Front

For the ordinary Party member, of course, the genuine enthusiasm which was felt in 1945 had as yet no cause for fundamental revision. On the domestic front – as Maurice Dobb's economic survey observed in October 1945 – much rebuilding was needed before higher living standards could become possible.[13]

Such expressions of tolerant understanding were by no means unusual and reflect the genuine goodwill of the Left, as well as its optimism that the trend in foreign policy might yet be reversed. Abroad there was, admittedly, already the problem of US support for the Kuomintang in China to worry about, not to mention British assistance for the forcible repossession of Vietnam and Indonesia by the former colonial powers. When the details of the American loan became known in December they were judged as evidence of the USA's 'increasingly open, aggressive, imperialist world role' but also as evidence of the defeat of 'the protagonists of a closed Empire bloc' in Britain – not all bad then, in short. In fact the Communists urged Labour to make the best of the 'short breathing space' afforded by these American dollars and to give priority to the 'drastic reorganisation of the British economy' – especially the basic industries.[14]

Throughout 1946 Labour's actual domestic reforms were judged positively. J.R. Campbell – in his time a thorn in the flesh of more than one Labour Government – complained only that the unions were not doing enough to encourage production drives in industry, but the Communist miners' leader, Arthur Horner, looked forward to a 'new team spirit' emerging on the coalfields because of nationalisation; it was not Socialism, he admitted, but it was 'a progressive and important stage in the march towards greater productive efficiency'.[15] Willie Gallacher, the Communist MP for West Fife, reviewed the Government's first year even more positively:

> What a change for the erstwhile overlords, for those who had come to think of themselves as the divinely appointed rulers of the country ... Now they speak in an atmosphere that is completely beyond their reckoning. Their pretensions are laughed at, their posturing is greeted with derision and scorn.[16]

But if this gives us an accurate picture of the solidarity

which Attlee's government commanded throughout the Labour Movement, and some flavour of the real sense of achievement and momentous change which it inspired, the Left's critique of Labour's foreign policy is no less important in reminding us that the war generated expectations of a socialist foreign policy and of friendship with the Soviet Union that were being dashed. On this issue Labour Left journals such as *Tribune* were if anything more consistently radical than the Communists – until, that is, the announcement of Marshall Aid in June 1947 – and it was a group of Labour Socialists who produced the most systematic indictment of the Government's policy when *Keep Left* was published earlier in that year.[17] In this rather prescient pamphlet, British foreign policy was depicted as an attempt to save the Empire by means of an anti-Communist alliance with the USA, which was expected to provide the necessary dollars; the world, meanwhile, would be divided into two mutually hostile camps.

Growing Criticism of Labour

By the autumn of 1947 the long-threatened polarisation of international relations had become an accomplished fact. President Truman's 'containment' speech, the European Recovery Programme, and the formation of the Communist Information Bureau were its final steps. 1947 was also significant as the year when Labour's reform programme lost momentum and socialist direction. It was thus possible, as well as necessary, for Communists to reappraise the totality of reforms already in place. To assist this process they were reminded by the leading Stalinist economist, Eugene Varga, that the context was 'the general crisis of capitalism' and that in response to this crisis Labour had effected a 'state capitalist' adaptation of the economy designed to prolong the rule of the bourgeoisie.[18]

This instantly raised doubts concerning Pollitt's confident

assertion in *Looking Ahead*, also published in 1947, 'that the essence of the period we are now in is that of a transition stage to Socialism'. Dutt was quick to conclude from Varga's analysis that nationalisation was 'no more than a legal device' characteristic of monopoly capitalism irrespective of its political forms – liberal, conservative, labour or fascist.[19]

But Varga was not finished. Some months later, perhaps with Soviet-dominated Eastern Europe in mind, he added that 'bourgeois nationalisation also signifies progress in the direction of the new type of democracy'.[20] The result was that the Communists were caught in a deeply equivocal formal view of Labour's domestic achievements simultaneously finding evidence of progressive advance and of the perpetuation of monopoly capitalism.[21] But in practice the position was much clearer; Labour, it was said, had not taken nationalisation far enough and had loosened central controls when it should have been tightening and extending them.[22]

Cold War

Meanwhile the international situation continued to deteriorate, reaching its nadir with the Korean War at the end of Labour's term of office. The Communists ceaselessly polemicised against the Marshall Plan as a device for American hegemony in Europe and the exploitation of workers.[23] From the autumn of 1947 they also began to relish the signs of an approaching economic slump and expected the USA to fall victim to 'the greatest crisis of overproduction the world has ever seen'.[24]

Stafford Cripps's austerity programme, in this view, was simply the sealing of 'the alliance' between right-wing Labour and big business in a vain attempt to solve the crisis at the expense of the workers. Labour's colonial policies – from the war against Communist insurgency in Malaya to the groundnuts scheme in Tanganyika – were denounced as uniformly imperialist,[25] while its election programme for

1950 was dismissed as 'an insult to the intelligence of the working class' – 'fraudulent' even by Liberal-Tory standards of old.[26]

Communist opposition to the Marshall Plan across the whole of Europe and the insistence that European recovery under its auspices could only mean an intensification of work and reductions in real pay, alerted governments everywhere to the prospect of renewed and bitter industrial conflict under Communist leadership. In Britain not only was support for the Labour government exceptionally strong within the TUC, the Marshall Plan was perceived by many on the left as a road to full employment rather than the economic slump and poverty predicted by the Communists. Thus the scene was set for the Party's isolation on this issue. When industrial conflict occurred after 1947, as it did, particularly in mining, transport, engineering, metals and shipbuilding, it tended to involve relatively short, unofficial stoppages which were increasingly explained as the result of a Communist conspiracy to sabotage the European Recovery Programme. Though the idea of conscious orchestration could not be supported with any evidence, Communists naturally exercised local leadership in many of these disputes in a context characterised by economic austerity, wage restraint, the use of compulsory arbitration and other forms of coercion (including prosecution of strikers). Communist shop stewards could hardly fail to exert some influence in these circumstances, but the alliances formed were not strong enough to prevent the purge of Communists from official positions in certain unions, as the General Council of the TUC recommended in 1948.

When in 1950 the TUC voted to reject the Government's policy of wage restraint, and when a year later the General Council called on the Government to repeal order 1305, under which strikers had been prosecuted, Communists could claim vindication of their industrial policies. Nevertheless the reality was that the Party had few friends beyond its own organisation once the Cold War got under way; even

Labour Left journals such as *Tribune* and the *New Statesman* joined the chorus of denunciation.

Thus by the time the Conservative Party returned to office in 1951, the high hopes and good will of 1945 had turned to bitter enmity. When the Government launched its offensive against the Communists in 1948 the party concluded that Labour was guilty of nothing less than 'the betrayal of Britain'. In order to preserve its global power, or so the Marxists reasoned, the British establishment had not only sacrificed domestic reconstruction by squandering colossal resources in policing the globe, it had done so as a junior partner of American imperialism, much as *Keep Left* had predicted in May 1947.[27] Many years earlier Georgi Dimitrov, one of the principal authors of the Popular Front strategy, had advised Harry Pollitt of the need for the Communists to 'look after the national honour of [your] country'.[28] Under Stalin's direction, the Communists now sought to play the national card against the USA and its stooges in Britain who had purportedly reduced the nation to the status of a colony. Communists now railed against the 'poisonous filth' of American comic strips, films, digests, novels – all manner of cultural imports which had allegedly 'reached appalling depths of degradation, sadism, neurosis, sensationalism, and scarcely veiled pornography'.[29] All over Europe, according to the Communists, social democracy had been the 'principal agency of American ideological penetration and propaganda', as well as its willing imperialist partner. But by 1951 the argument was not really about Labour at all – it was about the noxious international role of the USA. The trouble for the British Communists was that in the 'haunt of fears' which both sides generated there was no bigger bogey by 1951 than Stalin and the Soviet Union.[30]

Communist Party membership had fallen from its peak in 1942-3 even before the war had ended. But the international situation was the principal factor in marginalising the Party after June 1947. A witch hunt against Communists in the USA began that autumn, and the following years were replete with crises which threatened war – the Communist takeover in Czechoslovakia, the subsequent mysterious death of Jan Masaryk, the Socialist Foreign Minister, the Berlin Blockade, Tito's rebellion against Stalin, the Communist insurgency in Malaya, Mao's triumph in China and the Korean War. This pattern of encroachments by Communists continued without relief during the remaining months of the Labour governments. The British Party completely accepted the Soviet view of all these flash-points – events which, in Eastern Europe in particular, led to the elimination of the non-Communist left; and this was not the least factor in explaining the CPGB's loss of its Socialist allies by 1951. It is hardly surprising that there was widespread disbelief when the Party announced, in the same year, that it was committed to a new, democratic programme – *The British Road to Socialism*.

Notes

[1] P.M.H. Bell, *John Bull and the Bear: British Public Opinion, Foreign Policy, and the Soviet Union*, Edward Arnold, London 1990, passim.
[2] Editorial, *Modern Quarterly*, new series, 1, 1 December 1945, p1.
[3] *Ibid*, p4.
[4] R. Palme Dutt, Notes of the Month, *Labour Monthly* (henceforward *LM*), August 1945, p230; his earlier support for the coalition is expressed in his Notes of April and May 1945 in the same journal, p101 and p137 respectively.
[5] J. Gollan, 'Is "Modern Economics" Adequate?', *Modern Quarterly*, 1, 2 March 1946, p43.
[6] CPGB, *Communist Election Policy*, CPGB 1945, p6.
[7] R. Palme Dutt, Notes of the Month, *LM*, September 1945, p267 and p259-60; compare with his 'Whither India?', *LM*, June 1948, p165.
[8] H. Pollitt, *Looking Ahead*, CPGB 1947, p87.
[9] R. Palme Dutt, 'India – What Must Be Done?', *LM*, September 1942, pp259 and 266.
[10] R. Palme Dutt, Notes, *LM*, March 1942, p73.
[11] H. Pollitt, 'Lessons of the Labour Conference', *LM*, January 1945, p24.
[12] R. Palme Dutt, Notes, *LM*, September 1945, pp265-6.
[13] M. Dobb, 'The Economic Situation and Labour Policy', *LM*, October 1945, pp300-302.

[14] R. Palme Dutt, Notes, *LM*, January 1946, pp8-9 and p11.

[15] J.R. Campbell, 'Where Is The Production Drive'?, *LM*, June 1946, pp171-2; A. Horner, 'Nationalisation of the Coal Industry', *LM*, February 1946, pp44-5.

[16] W. Gallacher, 'A Year of Labour Government', *LM*, August 1946, p235.

[17] R.H.S. Crossman, M. Foot and I. Mikardo, *Keep Left*, New Statesman pamphlet, May 1947; see also, J. Schneer, *Labour's Conscience*, Unwin Hyman, London 1988.

[18] E. Varga, 'The General Crisis of Capitalism', *LM*, February 1947, p57 and p60.

[19] R. Palme Dutt, 'Lessons of the Crisis', *LM*, March 1947, p72.

[20] E. Varga, 'Democracy of a New Type', *LM*, August 1947, p237.

[21] R. Palme Dutt, Notes, *LM*, July 1948, pp196-7.

[22] J.R. Campbell, 'More Planning, More Democracy', *LM*, May 1947, pp142-6; M. Heinemann and N.J. Klugmann, 'Britain's Economic Strategy', *Modern Quarterly*, Spring 1947, pp148-51.

[23] M. Hudson, 'The Marshall Standard of Life', *LM*, October 1948, pp380-383.

[24] R. Palme Dutt, 'Britain's Crisis and World Crisis', *LM*, October 1947, pp295-6; Pollitt's prediction is contained in *Report of the Twenty-First Congress of the CPGB*, CPGB November 1949, p10.

[25] R. Palme Dutt, *Britain's Crisis of Empire*, Lawrence and Wishart, London 1949, passim.

[26] W. Gallacher, 'What A Programme!', *LM*, April 1949, p170; see also the same author's 'Next Year's Election', *LM*, June 1949, p334.

[27] R. Palme Dutt, 'The Betrayal of Britain', *LM*, January 1949, p6.

[28] F. King and G. Matthews (eds), *About Turn: The Communist Party and the Outbreak of the Second World War*, Lawrence and Wishart, London 1990, p209.

[29] A. Bush, 'Tasks of Cultural Workers', *Communist Review*, February 1951, p54; see also R. Palme Dutt's 'The Fight For British Independence' in the same issue, pp43-4.

[30] For an extended discussion of this anti-Americanism see M. Barker, *A Haunt of Fears*, Pluto, London 1984, pp25-6.

Defeat and Renewal: The Ideology of the Right

Martin Durham

> The overwhelming electoral defeat of 1945 shook the Conservative Party out of its lethargy and impelled it to rethink its philosophy and re-form its ranks with a thoroughness unmatched for a century.
>
> R.A. Butler, *The Art of the Possible*, Hamish Hamilton, London, 1971, p126.

The election of a Labour government in 1945 came as a massive shock to British Conservatives. Accustomed to government, presided over by a war leader who fully expected the support of a grateful population, Conservatives could hardly conceive of the possibility of electoral defeat. Yet this is precisely what befell them and in the years that followed the Party underwent a far-reaching process of organisational and ideological renewal before it was to escape the unfamiliar trammels of opposition and once again secure office. This process of renewal has already been the subject of substantial discussion elsewhere and it would not be possible here to explore many of the issues raised by these studies.[1] Instead, I shall focus on two important areas.

Firstly, what were the key themes in the ideological argument deployed by the Conservative Party against the 1945-51 Labour governments and in what ways did they shift during the period? And secondly, what was the relationship between the Party, the ideology it espoused and a British Right which it overwhelmingly dominated but did not completely define? An examination of these questions, I would suggest, will take us some considerable way in understanding how what one leading Conservative has recently called 'the oldest party in the world and probably the universe'[2] responded to the horrors of political defeat. Thirty years later, faced with economic decline and the apparent failure of collectivism, Conservatives were to turn to an uncomfortable mixture of market solutions and moralist rhetoric. But in 1945, having presided first over substantial unemployment in the 1930s and then a wartime Coalition government that had markedly increased Labour's prestige, no such option presented itself. The reshaping of Conservatism in the late 1940s was significantly different from the more familiar mutation associated with the rise three decades later of Margaret Thatcher.

Consensus and Conflict

British politics from the 1940s to the 1970s was dominated by a set of assumptions about government responsibility for full employment, state welfare provision and the coexistence of public and private enterprise that could fairly be called a cross-party consensus. But this did not entail complete agreement nor did it preclude very different emphases in the pronouncements of the leading parties. In an important sense, the period of the Attlee government is one of the forging of a 'New Conservatism' that explicitly broke with laissez-faire and embraced an expanded role for the State. However, this did not mean that the Party saw itself as in agreement with Labour. On the contrary, evoking libertarian themes of individualism and enterprise (and Tory themes of nation and Empire), post-war Conservatism fought what it insisted in calling 'the Socialist Party' as if the nation's life depended on it.

While there continues to be dispute about its extent, it is clear that the experience of coalition and of war economy

101

shifted Conservative opinion in the direction of a converging policy with its Labour partners. This remained the case after the coalition came to an end and the 1945 Conservative election manifesto accepted full employment, welfare provision and a National Health Service. The Party's election campaign, however, was more concerned with attempting to present Labour as extremist and a threat to liberty, with one Conservative candidate even claiming that, 'The socialist state of Cripps is to be the same as the Fascist state of the blackshirts'.[3] Nor was such a view unrepresentative. It was merely a reworking of Churchill's own claim, during his first radio broadcast of the campaign, that Socialism was 'inseparably interwoven with totalitarianism' and that a Labour government, to implement its policies, would have to fall back upon 'some kind of Gestapo', a claim that received the retort from Attlee that it represented a second-hand rendition of the views of 'an Austrian professor, Friedrich August von Hayek'.[4]

This rendering of the fears encapsulated the previous year in Hayek's *The Road to Serfdom* did not save the Party from defeat at the hands of an electorate unpersuaded of Conservatism's reforming credentials. In the aftermath of Labour's victory, advocates of modernising the Party, both organisationally and ideologically, found a chastened and receptive audience. Crucially, they believed, it was necessary to educate the Party activist – and the unconvinced voter – that Conservatives did not reject planning. Indeed it was proudly claimed in a pamphlet produced by the Party after the 1945 defeat that pre-war Britain had been a regulated society, presided over by an interventionist administration.[5] Leading Conservatives, most notably 'Rab' Butler, were insistent that laissez-faire had been but an interlude and that 'positive guidance by the State' was central to British tradition. In nineteenth century social legislation, he declared, and in inter-war tariffs on imports and intervention in the economy could be seen the true face of British Conservatism.[6] This educational endeavour culminated in 1947 in the

Industrial Charter which proclaimed that the nature of modern industry and the situation in which the country found itself necessitated 'strong central guidance', insisting that the Party believed not only in government responsibility for a high rate of employment but that jobs should be available 'to all who are willing to work'.[7] For the Labour Left paper, *Tribune*, such a policy represented a defeat of the Tory Party and Tory philosophy – 'it makes sense only if the Conservative Party sees its future as a kind of moderate wing of the Labour Party which accepts all the major proposals of the Labour Government but concentrates on criticism in detail – as a sort of *Keep Right* group'.[8] Comparable views were to be found on the right. For the *Daily Express*, the Charter was 'infected by Socialist ideas'[9] while at the 1947 Conservative Conference one dissident MP, Sir Waldron Smithers, characterised it as 'milk and water socialism', urging those present to save both Party and country by rejecting it.[10]

The passing of the Charter at the 1947 Conference represented a defeat for those who believed that Labour's advance could be beaten back without accepting the fundamental shift in popular expectations and the boundaries of the politically possible. In *The Case for Conservatism*, published in the same year, the Conservative MP Quintin Hogg demonstrated how far the ground had shifted by not only arguing against the view that laissez-faire had ever 'been good Conservative doctrine', but also drawing attention to the degree to which the two manifestos of 1945 had been in agreement, calling upon the party to take up the banner of 'social democracy … and a planned economy' in the battle to restore its electoral fortunes.[11]

Set the People Free

The vote in support of the Industrial Charter and the views expressed by Hogg, significantly a wartime advocate of Tory support for social reform, represented a high-water mark for the most radical interpretation of 'the New Conservatism'. The economic problems that the Labour government was now facing, the potential popularity of opposition to rationing and controls and, no doubt, the urgings of business organisations, gave renewed purchase to an approach that attacked both social democracy and planning. Here, claims of totalitarianism were crucial. Churchill's speech to the 1947 Conservative Conference claimed that Labour government restrictions on travel, its plans for the direction of labour and its level of taxation meant that 'on every side and by every means the machinery for the totalitarian grip upon British society' was 'being built up and perfected'.[12] As part of a renewed Conservative offensive, this claim was to be made with particular force in the Party's 1951 election manifesto, which took the form of a personal statement by Churchill in which he declared 'we must guard the British way of life, hallowed by centuries of tradition' against the destruction of freedom inevitable under a Socialist State. In 1949, in a question and answer section of a publication aimed at party activists, it was asked how Churchill's claim about the Gestapo could be believed. The reply was that full Socialism had not yet been introduced – another term in office could well result in the same suppression of opposition as was occurring in eastern Europe.[13]

How important were such claims to Party propaganda? Do they give grounds to abandon the suggestion that Labour and Conservative had substantially converged? The most important policy pronouncements following the passing of the Industrial Charter show a complex picture.

In *The Right Road for Britain*, which appeared in mid-1949, the Party positioned itself as the champion of liberty, enterprise and the individual. Socialism, it was argued, favoured centralisation and interference in private life and, regardless of what Socialists might intend, laid the ground for Communism. Conservatism, conversely, stood for individual personality, 'private thrift and house-ownership' and the release of 'initiative in the economic field'. Much of this stark contrast was muted in the detail. Government powers of taxation and over currency, it was argued, could be used to 'guide the economic activity of the country', and controls over foreign exchange or food rationing could not be abandoned while the nation remained in crisis. Nor, while iron and steel would not be nationalised and road goods haulage would be returned to the private sector, would the public ownership of other industries be reversed. The Social Services, too, received support, the Party pledging to 'endeavour faithfully to maintain the range and scope of these Services, and the rates of benefits.'[14] The Party, it was evident, accepted much of post-war Britain, but insisted that only it could retain welcome reforms while protecting the citizen and expanding the economy.

In the following year, in *This is the Road*, the Party's election manifesto, the intention to 'bring Nationalization to a full stop here and now' was reiterated, increased housing promised as basic to a property-owning democracy (a key notion introduced into the post-war Party by Anthony Eden) and reductions in state expenditure put forward as the road to lower taxation. As soon as possible, it was pledged, 'we shall abolish the existing rationing system.' Yet rather than deepening the emphasis on freedom, the contrast was more one of efficiency against incompetence and, still conscious of the shifted ground on which it now stood, the Party promised both to maintain and improve the National Health Service and to treat 'the maintenance of full employment as the first aim of a Conservative Government.'[15]

For the 1951 General Election the Party issued two documents, a 3000 word manifesto and a 10,000 word statement of policy. Written under the shadow of the Korean War, the emphasis of the longer document was on Socialist weakness in the face of Communist attack. Both freedom and efficiency could be intermingled in this account, in which a section entitled 'Peace through Strength' was followed by one entitled 'Strength through Enterprise'. The first, amidst its concerns with rearmament and defence treaties, urged that it be made clear to the peoples of central and eastern Europe that their loss of political freedom would be reversed, while also declaring the Party's intent to counter Communist propaganda by convincing 'the Colonial peoples' that their future lay in self-government within the British Empire. The second section, working through the well-worn proposals of selective denationalisation, public spending cuts and lower taxes, was not unsurprisingly followed by a discussion of 'Freedom and Security', in which the quintessential Tory theme of society as 'no mere collection of individuals' but a fellowship involving duties was invoked in order to present the social services as an expression of this fellowship, with initiative and enterprise as the essential preconditions for producing the wealth without which such services would founder.[16]

The Party that was elected to office in 1951, while embracing the collectivist trinity of full employment, welfare and a significant nationalised sector, had found a way of retaining and even reviving the older themes of individualism and nationalism. In so doing, it could gain from the electoral collapse of the Liberal Party (down from over 2.5 million to under 750,000) and revive the appeal of Conservatism to its own dispirited following. But it could also gain from the absence of any other significant political vehicle on the Right.

Free Marketeers and Fascists

This was most obviously the case with Fascism, never a serious challenge to Conservatism in Britain and now crippled by popular hostility to the regimes which the country had just fought. Towards the end of the war, an attempt to bring together elements of the extreme Right in the National Front after Victory proved unsuccessful and while some pre-war groupings persisted, most far Right activity took place in small and localised Mosleyite groupings, only brought together in 1948 with the launch of the Union

Movement. While adopting a name that deliberately retained a link to the pre-war British Union (of Fascists), Mosley's new movement claimed to have moved beyond Fascism and now stood not for British nationalism but for European Union. Much, however, remained the same, as might be suggested by Mosley's publication in 1946 of a new edition of his pre-war National Socialist text, *Tomorrow We Live*, with its proposals for a Corporate State, its characterisation of Jews as Orientals who had no place in Britain and its attacks on the British party system as a tool of international finance. Despite some incidents of street violence, the British far Right made little impact either on the media or the public.[17]

More important were the free marketeers of the Society of Individualists (from 1947 the Society for Individual Freedom), though less for the press reports of its luncheons and the publications of its letters in the national and local press than for the presence of supporters on the Conservative backbenches. This was not without its problems, its leading figure, Sir Ernest Benn, worrying that some of his colleagues 'unless kept strictly in hand, would turn us into a subsidiary of the Conservative Party.' Their idea, he feared, was 'to use us in the work of turning out the Government and they are not a bit interested in the more important work of rooting Socialism out of the Conservative Party.'[18] The Society's propaganda did present an alternative to the Conservative mainstream, but the body proved unable either to break free of Tory links or secure a significant following. The same might be said of other anti-socialist organisations of the period, such as the Economic League and Aims of Industry. With them, however, a single-minded concentration on criticism of the Labour Movement was exactly what was wanted.

As the Economic League noted in its Annual Report for 1950, its concern was to promote economic understanding 'from the standpoint that ... The preservation of personal freedom and free enterprise is essential to national well-being', adding that, while non-party, it would 'actively oppose all subversive forces ... that seek to undermine the security of Britain in general and British industry in particular.' In pursuit of that aim, the League during that year 'held over 19,000 meetings, distributed 18,000,000 leaflets, and obtained more than 30,000 column inches of press publicity. Leaflet subjects included ... Risk in Free Enterprise ... Menace of Communism ... Nationalisation and the Sheffield "Peace Congress".'[19]

Other bodies were also active, for instance the Institute of Directors, likewise emphasising its non-party nature, launched a Free Enterprise Campaign in 1951 focusing on 'the *choice* which it gives the consumer and the *chance* which it gives the employee to get on'.[20] But by far the most important orgnisation was Aims of Industry, which played a crucial part in the successful campaign by Tate and Lyle (utilising such slogans as TATE NOT STATE) to resist Labour proposals for the nationalisation of the sugar industry. Established in 1942, Aims by 1950 was backed by over 2,000 companies, placing during that year over 90,000 column inches of propaganda in newspapers in addition to providing speakers for meetings and supplying material for parliamentary questions.[21] The most notable of its activities may well have been its dispatch of trucks around the country, showing films to audiences outside factory gates and elsewhere, but it was perhaps even more imaginative in its supply of articles to the press with such titles as 'Why No Homes For Newly-weds?', 'Don't Nationalize Our Larders' and, referring to fears over law and order, 'For Those "Cosh" Boys – Bevan Must Share The Blame'. Ostensibly written by public figures (ranging from the President of the Master Builders Federation to the Chief Woman Officer of the Transport and General Workers Union), the articles were actually written by its staff.[22]

If the business organisations were allies, and Fascists posed no threat, Conservative hegemony on the British Right also gained from the rise and fall of the populist and highly unpredictable British Housewives' League. Founded in 1945, the Housewives' League in the early years of the Labour government appears to have gained a mass following which it was unable to maintain. Claiming some 100,000 members at its peak, the League concentrated its fire on government rationing and was able in its early stages to mobilise Labour voters among its serried ranks of angry women. This was not to last, however, and allegations of Tory links, although denied by both the League and the Conservatives, narrowed its appeal. Certainly the admitted funding of one meeting by the Road Haulage Federation cast doubt on its motives as did the presence of a prominent Conservative MP as one of the main speakers. If anything, however, the League stood to the right of the party, arguing in the first issue of its magazine that the Conservative government of the 1930s had paved the way for socialism and denouncing in its second issue Churchill's support for Beveridge and what it saw as the totalitarian implications of a nationalised health system. The League appears to have lost support rapidly, removing any possible threat it might have posed to the balance of forces on the Right, and further research is needed to disentangle the different strands of a movement which underwent several splits over its political direction. It seems best understood, however, through the declaration in a 1951 copy of its magazine that its members should not be seen as 'props for the Conservative Party. There is no doubt that all three Parties are seriously infiltrated with Fabianism'. By 1951, however, its depleted forces were in no position to act on this anti-Tory stance. Instead, it was Conservatism that benefited from the energies the League had summoned up in its fight against Labour controls.[23]

The forging of consensus between Labour and Conservative, substantial as it was, was no mere convergence. Instead the two parties remained fiercely antagonistic throughout the period. Able to encompass both economic liberals and what wartime Tory reformers had called 'the Progressive Right',[24] post-war Conservatism veered in the direction of the latter without abandoning the rhetoric and some of the policies which retained the support of the former. Such a strategy enabled the Party to preside over a mixed economy in the years that followed while never losing sight of the claim that it was doing so in a particularly national and conservative fashion. Free enterprise groups fought alongside it, however uncomfortably upon occasion, and with Liberals in disarray and radical Right marginalised, Conservative hegemony appeared safely ensconced; as, for thirteen years, it proved to be.

Notes

[1] J.D. Hoffman, *The Conservative Party in Opposition, 1945-51*, MacGibbon and Kee, London 1964; N. Harris, *Competition and the Corporate Society*, Methuen, London 1972, Part II; A. Gamble, *The Conservative Nation*, Routledge and Kegan Paul, London 1974, Ch 3; J. Ramsden, ' "A Party For Owners Or A Party For Earners?" How Far Did The British Conservative Party Really Change After 1945?', *Transactions of the Royal Historical Society*, Vol. 37, 1987, pp49-63; B. Schwarz, 'The Tide of History: the reconstruction of Conservatism, 1945-51' in N. Tiratsoo (ed), *The Attlee Years*, Pinter, London 1991.

[2] John Patten, Secretary of State of Education, in *The Guardian*, 8 October, 1992.

[3] P. Addison, *The Road to 1945*, Quartet, London 1977, pp264-5; A. Calder, *The People's War*, Panther, London 1971, p667.

[4] A. Sked and C. Cook, *Post-War Britain*, Penguin, London 1984; K.O. Morgan, *Labour in Power 1945-51*, Oxford University Press, Oxford, 1984, p39.

[5] W.H. Greenleaf, *The British Political Tradition*, Volume Two, Routledge, London 1983, pp256-7.

[6] *About the Industrial Charter*, extracted in *Conservatism 1945-1950*, Conservative Political Centre, London 1950, p47.

[7] *The Industrial Charter*, extracted in *ibid*, pp52, 59.

[8] *Tribune*, 16 May, 1947.

[9] *Daily Express*, 12 May, 1947.

[10] *68th Annual Conference: Verbatim Report*, National Union of Conservative and Unionist Associations, London 1947, pp49-50.

[11] Q. Hogg, *The Case for Conservatism*, Penguin, Harmondsworth 1947, pp229-33, 306.

[12] *68th Annual Conference, op.cit*, p117.

[13] F.W.S. Craig, *British General Election Manifestos, 1918-66*, Political Reference Publications, Chichester 1970, p144; *The Conservative Approach*, August, 1949.

[14] *The Right Road for Britain*, reprinted in *Conservatism 1945-50*, *op.cit.*, pp173-224; quotes from pp177, 183, 205.

[15] *This is the Road*, reprinted in *ibid.*, pp225-48; quotes from pp233, 235, 232. For the property-owning democracy, see the *Onlooker*, November, 1946.

[16] *Britain Strong and Free*, Conservative and Unionist Central Office, London 1951; quotes from pp12, 25.

[17] R. Thurlow, *Fascism in Britain*, Blackwell, Oxford, 1987, Ch10; L.S. Rose, *Fascism in Britain*, published by author, London 1948; O. Mosley, *My Answer*, Mosley Publications, Ramsbury 1946.

[18] D. Abel, *Ernest Benn*, Ernest Benn Ltd., London 1960, pp124-37; quotes from p131.

[19] A.A. Rogow and P. Shore, *The Labour Government and British Industry, 1945-1951*, Blackwell, Oxford 1955, p146.

[20] Ibid., pp147-8.

[21] H.H. Wilson, 'Techniques of Pressure: Anti-Nationalization Propaganda in Britain', *Public Opinion Quarterly*, Summer 1951, pp227-8; H.G. Nicholas, *The British General Election of 1950*, Macmillan, London 1951, p72; Rogow and Shore, *op.cit.*, pp144-5.

[22] Wilson, *op.cit.*, pp229-30.

[23] B. Campbell, *The Iron Ladies*, Virago, London 1987, pp76-82; *Times*, 3 July, 1947; *Housewives Today*, April, June, 1947, March, 1951. For a fuller account of the Housewives League see article by James Hinton in *History Workshop Journal*, Number 38, 1995.

[24] Gamble, *op.cit.*, p34.

111

Part 2 – A Welfare Society?

The Welfare State: a New Society?

John Callaghan

There are some to whom the pursuit of security appears to be a wrong aim. They think of security as something inconsistent with initiative, adventure, personal responsibility. This is not a just view of Social Security as planned in this Report. The plan is not one for giving to everybody something for nothing and without trouble, or something that will free the recipients forever thereafter from personal responsibilities. The plan is one to secure income for subsistence on condition of service and contribution and in order to make and keep men fit for service.

Beveridge Report, Paragraph 455, 1942.

Total war can generate the mixture of idealism and expediency conducive to social reform. It illuminates social problems, generates some of its own and creates crisis circumstances which cause these problems to be seen from the perspective of national efficiency and social solidarity. It augments the role of government, breaks the rules of economic orthodoxy and that 'dull conformity of everyday life' which normally inhibits popular demands for radical change.[1] The Second World War, furthermore, was fought in the name of democracy against fascist totalitarianism. It contained elements of a 'People's War', and there is clear evidence that by the autumn of 1942 'a major upheaval in public opinion had taken place'.[2]

This shift to the left ensured that social reform would have to figure in plans for post-war reconstruction, and it was popular acclaim for the Beveridge Report of 1942 which overcame Tory and official scepticism. Mention of such obstructions is a reminder that however propitious the wartime context was for raising social reform on the political agenda, the active element in politics was decisive in both shaping its content and seeing it through. Labour actually possessed distinctive ideas in the field of social policy and did not merely enter office in 1945 with the fruits of a war-generated consensus fallen into its lap, though for propaganda purposes the Attlee government was often at pains to stress the consensual nature of its reforms.[3]

The Background to Beveridge

But it is with the Beveridge Report on *Social Insurance and Allied Services* that one has to begin – that unlikely best-seller to which the term 'welfare state' was instantly attached and which, according to a Gallup poll conducted within two weeks of its publication, 90 per cent of the population wanted to see adopted.[4] Its principal objective, in the words of the report, was 'to abolish want by ensuring that every citizen willing to serve according to his powers has at all times an income sufficient to meet his responsibilities'. It was to achieve this goal via six main proposals: the maintenance of full employment (assuming an average unemployment rate of 8½ per cent), a unified health system, family allowances, a uniform system of National Insurance, abolition of poor relief and the payment of subsistence level benefits. Because these proposals were to cover everyone irrespective of income and to guarantee a 'national minimum' as of right, they were later said to embody a new conception of social citizenship.[5] Certainly the research which Beveridge commissioned – the Nuffield College Reconstruction Survey supervised by G.D.H. Cole in 1942 – provided evidence of overwhelming dislike of the niggardly, narrow and coercive system which his report was supposed to sweep away.[6]

The view expressed was virtually unanimous that pre-war

benefit levels were hopelessly inadequate, that claimants hated means testing and were ignorant of their rights. Respondents placed health at the top of their demands for future reform and particularly objected to the exclusion of wives and children from the existing health insurance scheme. The majority believed that the 'panel' system provided only inferior health care and that its doctors were overburdened with patients. They found the administrative procedures of the Assistance Boards, which administered the 'dole', hostile and demoralising – with respondents complaining about an official environment obsessed with breaches of the regulations. It was the same in the Labour Exchanges; during the inter-war years, 'they were regarded by the unemployed as enemy territory' – 'dingy and repellant to the eye', chairs bolted to the floor, officials – no doubt prodded from above to detect malingerers – always suspicious and interrogatory.[7] Only 20 per cent of adult vacancies were filled through the Labour Exchanges in any case, and the unemployed had reason to believe that they were subject to a 'futile and brutal ritual'.

But the system which the working class unemployed disliked so much was not without its uses. The dole was the cheapest way that successive Tory governments – obsessed with 'sound money' and utterly opposed to the creation of jobs by state intervention – could deal with unemployment. As Ross McKibbin argues in the work quoted above, the dole maintained a politically marginalised client population, wearied by futile conflict with the dole administration and easily coerced by threats of withdrawal of payment. At the same time it provided the Tories with opportunities to 'confirm politically necessary stereotypes' through the public pursuit of the scrounger.[8] The size of the anti-Labour vote in these twenty years and the resulting one-party system of government – punctuated only by short-lived minority Labour administrations – is proof that the class stereotypes employed had resonance, not only in suburbia, but within the working class itself.[9]

The TUC, the Beveridge Report and the Labour Party

It is relevant, in the context of such stereotypes, to observe that even in the conditions of rising expectations of reform generated by the war, radical social policy proposals were few and far between. José Harris finds that the significance of the Beveridge Report 'lay much less in its substantive proposals than in its synthesis of secondary opinion' and the transmission of these ideas to an audience in which 'they had long been in vogue'.[10] The TUC representatives who gave evidence to the Beveridge Committee, for example, ultimately supported the Beveridgean synthesis. They approved of the contributory principle and found nothing to criticise in the regressive aspect of flat-rate contributions. There was no echo of the conflict which had followed Labour's acceptance of the Liberal contributory insurance scheme in 1911; on that occasion 'a substantial section of the parliamentary party, led by [Philip] Snowden, did not accept the proposal' – and the dissidents were supported by a majority at the Labour Party's Annual Conferences in 1912 and 1913.[11] The dissident case had stressed that the State should pay for social reform through progressive taxation to ensure that the burden fell on those best able to meet it; this approach also meant that the political problem of bringing about a major redistribution of income was faced squarely.[12] But in 1942 only a handful of constituency Labour Parties voiced this argument.

In fact the TUC delegation to the Beveridge Committee was not only strongly in favour of contributory insurance but surprised some of those assembled by speaking contemptuously of 'dodgers', of the 'very poor' and of 'the type of person who will not join a Friendly Society'.[13] The delegation also favoured the withdrawal of public assistance from the wives and children of workers who went on strike. Harris notes that all of this embodied 'the traditional sterling virtues of the labour aristocracy' but such prejudices also echo the 'politically necessary stereotypes' of the inter-war years and go some way to an understanding of why the Conservatives

118

were able to harvest up to 50 per cent of the working-class vote in that period; the Victorian ideology which explained poverty in terms of the individual shortcomings of the poor was far from dead. No witness to the Beveridge Committee raised the issue of those in need who were permanently outside the labour market and thus excluded from an insurance scheme based on individual flat-rate contributions. Yet, as has been noted, Beveridge himself assumed that post-war unemployment would average as much as 8½ per cent (the actual 1954 figure was 1.2 per cent – 280,000 persons). Meanwhile the central bureaucracy rejected the principle of subsistence benefits, questioned the need for family allowances and 'suggested that there was an irreducible class of hopeless, feckless persons for whom it would always be necessary to retain a large residual system of deterrent and disciplinary means-tested poor relief'.[14]

When the Beveridge Report was published it 'dovetailed almost perfectly with both Labour's rhetoric and its plans for social insurance' (adopted eighteen months earlier), and no major criticism of the scheme was found either in the statements of leading left-wing intellectuals such as R.H. Tawney, G.D.H. Cole and Harold Laski or in left-wing journals such as *Tribune* and the *New Statesman*.[15] Labour wanted substantial increases, however, on the rate of benefits proposed by Beveridge, as well they might. Though his proposals were criticised in Cabinet and at the Treasury for being 'shockingly extravagant', Maynard Keynes was nearer to the mark when he pronounced them 'the cheapest alternative open to us'.[16] As Harris points out,

> the definition of subsistence on which Beveridge's estimates of welfare benefits were based was deliberately kept to a very basic spartan minimum, partly to encourage private saving and partly to maintain the traditional Poor Law principle of a substantial incentive gap between wages and benefits – the so-called 'principle of less eligibility'.[17]

119

First, Beveridge calculated the cost on the assumption that all the benefits of universal cover were paid at subsistence level and then proceeded to amend his plan on the basis of what was deemed economically possible. This reduced the projected cost to one-fifth of the original sum. Though expedience played an undoubted part in this pruning Beveridge, as we have seen, also had other objectives in mind as well as the elimination of want. He rejected what he called 'the Santa Claus state' and believed throughout his life in the application of market criteria to state-provided social security.[18]

Social Welfare and the Machinery of State

The Education Act of 1944 which R.A. Butler steered through Parliament represented the other great area of social policy in which an attempt was made during the war to streamline and expand a ramshackle and begrudging pre-war order. It created the tripartite system of grammar, technical and secondary modern schools – which was later denounced by the Left as a mechanism for reproducing the class structure – and raised the school leaving age to fifteen. But Butler had fashioned an enabling Act which left a good deal of discretion to local authorities to decide which schools were actually provided in any area. Provision for technical and further education remained woefully inadequate, and so in this respect Butler's Platonic division of the population into three types failed to live up to its own expectations.[19] Attlee expressed concern in February 1944 that technical (as well as university) education was being neglected, but the ambiguities of Labour's approach to secondary education did not amount to a coherent alternative policy. The National Association of Labour Teachers favoured the comprehensive school – the multilateral as it was then known – and the Party's Annual Conference supported the idea in 1942. But there was also considerable support in the Party for the grammar school and the idea that gradual reform of the existing system would provide working-class children with more access to what was already regarded as excellent. Thus, in 1945 the Education Act was accepted as the basis for further reform by Labour's Annual Conference. When Ellen Wilkinson became Minister for Education, however, further reform was shelved. The counsel of officials prevailed in favour of implementing the established policy (in difficult circumstances, given the shortage of building materials) rather than the more radical opinion of interested pressure groups within the Party.[20]

Wilkinson's frustration with her departmental demands for rapid action, which left little time for reflection on education according to her biographer,[21] raises the larger question of her Party's attitude to the machinery of government. At the time of the Liberal reforms over thirty years earlier, considerable disquiet was expressed concerning the appearance of what Hilaire Belloc termed *The Servile State* (1912). Suspicion of the authoritarian implications of an enlarged state intervention was also voiced on the left – notably by syndicalists and guild socialists. But it was also evident within the socialist mainstream. Fred Jowett waged a campaign for constitutional reform for many years to strengthen the role of backbench MPs and managed to convert the Independent Labour Party to his scheme for a new committee structure of elected members in 1926; even Beatrice and Sidney Webb became opponents of the executive 'dictatorship' which functioned behind the fiction of Parliamentary sovereignty.[22] The would-be constitutional reformers failed, however, to shift the dominant complacency which characterised Labour's attitude to the British State. Indeed, the inter-war recession strengthened statist versions of socialism by simultaneously piling-up the agenda of necessary reforms which required state action and, at the same time, weakening the extra-parliamentary movement in which many of the reformers had placed their hopes for constitutional change.[23]

When constitutional issues next captured the attention of

the Left – after the 1931 political crisis – the overriding concern was to ensure that a future socialist majority could not be sabotaged by vested interests. The thrust of this thinking accordingly concerned itself with measures to strengthen the executive, strengthen party control of ministers and speed-up Parliamentary procedure.[24] The Left in the Labour Party, led intellectually by people such as Sir Stafford Cripps and Harold Laski, saw the class-based two-party system and the possibility it afforded of a clear-cut socialist majority in Parliament as the best way to advance their programme – a form of state collectivism. When Labour formed its first majority government in 1945 these anticipations seemed fulfilled – especially when one considers the size of the majority and the absence of any countervailing extra-parliamentary pressure for a more participatory democracy. The war experience, furthermore, could only have strengthened the feeling that the existing political arrangements could meet any test. The Labour Ministers in the coalition became especially conscious of the great powers of the State and expected to draw on the administrative experience it had acquired during the conflict. As Ben Pimlott notes in his biography of Hugh Dalton 'it was this discovery – epitomised in Douglas Jay's remark after the war that "the gentleman in Whitehall is usually right" – that found expression in Labour's election programme'.[25]

With relation to public ownership, a bureaucratic model held sway well before the war broke out; and it is perhaps revealing of the extent to which the change in ownership of certain industries was thought to be a sufficient stimulus in bringing to life a new ideal of public service, that Attlee later confessed this area of policy to have been his biggest disappointment – when the expected change failed to materialise.[26]

But in the field of health Labour did envisage democratic reform to involve British citizens. It had demanded nationalisation of the hospitals since before the First World War, but from 1922 Labour developed the idea of health centres, subject to local popular control, as the basis of a national health system providing a free service at the point of need. Salaried doctors would work in group practices from these health centres. The Socialist Medical Association (SMA) – another pressure group within the Party – played the main part in keeping these ideas alive in the 1930s. Local authorities were to administer the health centres and public hospitals on a regional basis. Regional health committees would implement national policy but were expected to be responsible to those they served. During the war, the Labour Party's Public Health Committee was dominated by members of the SMA and the idea of 'democratic control and public responsibility of the new regional health committees' remained a major emphasis – as evinced by the Party's *National Service For Health* (1943).[27]

Though the war years saw the question of health rise up the national agenda and attempts by the medical profession to influence the direction of future policy, neither Whitehall nor the doctors' organisations were ready to accept a salaried profession under local control, as proposed by Labour's health policy groups. Furthermore, once the Cabinet and its reconstruction committees turned to health reform in 1943 and 1944, Labour ministers in the coalition 'resolutely pursued the Party's distinctive concerns' in this area.[28] They were unsuccessful, however, in getting these concerns into the coalition's White Paper *A National Health Service* (February 1944) which Labour accepted only as an interim measure. By November 1945 it was clear that the Labour Minister of Health, Aneurin Bevan, intended to introduce a more radical reform than his Conservative predecessor Henry Willink. But it was also less radical than the plan proposed by the SMA. Bevan's draft scheme gave emphasis to group partnerships working from health centres, the nationalisation of hospitals under regional boards accountable to his department and a salaried component in the pay of general practitioners.

Within Cabinet these proposals were criticised for eroding local control of hospitals. Outside government, the Left was dismayed to find that Bevan had tried to buy the co-operation of the British Medical Association (BMA) by allowing private practice to continue within the National Health Service and by agreeing to retain capitation fees as the basis of doctors' income. Despite these concessions – and the fact that the doctors were to be permitted a dominant role in health administration – the BMA continued to oppose the scheme well after it was introduced into law in May 1946. Two years later Bevan was still having to appease its opposition to a salaried service and allay its fears of political control (local or central) of the profession. But, by the time the NHS Act became operative in July 1948, between a quarter and a third of general practitioners had joined the scheme in the various regions of Britain. By vesting day only 10 per cent remained outside, but the decisive statistic is surely the fact that 97 per cent of the population were enrolled within a few months of the 'appointed day'.

The NHS was the most important social reform of the Attlee government, despite Bevan's forced retreat and the fact that locally-controlled health centres were never to occupy the central role envisaged by the SMA. It was, as Rudolf Klein expressed it, 'the first health system in any Western society to offer free medical care to the entire population [and] ... the first ... to be based not on the insurance principle ... but on the national provision of services available to everyone'.[29] For Bevan himself it was 'pure Socialism' in this sense, but flawed even in his own mind not only by the existence of 'pay beds', but by the practice of ministerial nomination of appointments to its various administrative bodies.[30] By the time he came to write *In Place of Fear* (1952), he wanted the electoral principle to encroach on the NHS bureaucracy, though having opted for a national, rather than a local, form of state control he admitted that it was not obvious how this could be achieved. The more pressing battle, however, and one which eventually led to Bevan's resignation from the Government, was over NHS funding. By April 1951 the nagging issue of rising NHS expenditure in the context of economic austerity was resolved